UNLESS YOU REPENT

H. A. IRONSIDE

Books by H. A. Ironside

The Daily Sacrifice
Four Hundred Silent Years
Holiness: The False and the True
Wrongly Dividing the Word of Truth
A Historical Sketch of the Brethren Movement
H. A. Ironside's Bible Commentaries include volumes on:
Joshua, Ezra, Nehemiah, Esther
Psalms (1-41)
Proverbs, Song of Solomon
Isaiah
Jeremiah, Lamentations
Ezekiel
Daniel
The Minor Prophets
Matthew
Mark
Luke
John
Acts
Romans
1 Corinthians
2 Corinthians
Galatians, Ephesians
Philippians, Colossians, Thessalonians
1 & 2 Timothy, Titus, Philemon
Hebrews, James, 1 & 2 Peter
1 & 2 & 3 John, Jude
Revelation

UNLESS YOU REPENT

H. A. IRONSIDE

GOSPEL FOLIO PRESS
304 Killaly St. West Port Colborne, ON L3K 6A6

Published by Gospel Folio Press
304 Killaly St. West Port Colborne, ON L3K 6A6

Originally published in 1937 by American Tract Society
as *Except Ye Repent*

ISBN 1-882701-07-0

Cover design by J. B. Nicholson, Jr.

Printed in the United States of America

I am not come to call the
righteous, but sinners to repentance.
MATTHEW 9:13

Except ye repent, ye shall all likewise perish.
LUKE 13:3

Joy shall be in heaven over one sinner that repenteth.
LUKE 15:7

Repent ye, therefore, and be converted, that your sins may be blotted out.
ACTS 3:19

Foreword

It is a tribute to Dr. Ironside's books that they are still in demand even if he, himself, has been with the Lord since 1951.

It is especially timely that his book, *Unless You Repent,* should be reprinted at this time. It deals with issues that are the subject of some misinformation and misunderstanding.

First of all, there is a strong effort to redefine repentance. Some good and godly teachers hold that it only means a changed attitude toward God and the Lord Jesus Christ. They resist any attempt to define it as a turning away from sin.

Linked with that is the insistence that, since salvation is by faith alone, repentance from sin must not be included in the gospel message. The reason for this is a fear that repentance becomes a work, whereas we know that salvation is "not of works."

Actually, repentance *is* a work, but it is not a *meritorious* work. Even faith is a work. Jesus said, "This is the work of God, that you believe in Him whom He sent" (John 6:29). But it is not a work that gives a person merit for heaven. Repentance and faith are like two sides of a coin. One side is "repentance toward God" and the other side is "faith in our Lord Jesus Christ" (Acts 20:21). To exercise saving faith, a person must first acknowledge that he is ungodly.

Dr. Ironside's clear and gracious handling of the subject comes as a breath of fresh air, dispelling the fog.

WILLIAM MACDONALD
July 19, 1994

7

Publisher's Preface

When the American Tract Society first asked for a "treatise on one or more essential evangelical doctrines of the Christian faith," little did they realize that H. A. Ironside would send them an explosive manuscript that would lay bare what is popularly called "easy believism."

Here is his most muscular work. A feisty book for any who soften the gospel of our Lord Jesus Christ. Still, in the heat of battle, our brother remained a gentleman. He had no intention of blackening anyone's character or ministry.

H. A. Ironside was uniquely qualified to give the clarion call about repentance. He was first a fruitful evangelist, and secondly, a thorough, intelligent Bible teacher. How rarely do we see these gifts of evangelist and teacher combined. Besides this, he has given us volumes that are unimpeachable in their orthodoxy, and command the respect of the Church of God. He had seen the drift of the evangelical church, and in this book we read his farseeing warning.

Those who minimize the preaching of repentance, or worse, banish it altogether, are left with scanty ground to stand after reading *Unless You Repent.* All the opposers could do in response was give the silent treatment. This classic on the doctrine of repentance has unfortunately been largely ignored by the fundamentalist movement, and by the evangelical movement that has sprung out of fundamentalism.

Ironside knew when he wrote the book that he was a voice in the wilderness. By God's enabling, he stood up to face that chill north wind with a message both impassioned and eloquent.

Contents

Introduction

Fully convinced in my own mind that the doctrine of repentance is the missing note in many otherwise orthodox and fundamentally sound circles, I have penned this volume out of a full heart. I hope and pray that God will be pleased to use it to awaken many of His servants to the importance of seeking to present His truth in the way that will bring men to the only place where He can meet them in blessing. That place is the recognition of their own demerit and absolute unworthiness of His mercies and a new conception of His saving power for all who come to Christ as lost sinners. There they must rest alone on His redemptive work for salvation and depend on the indwelling Holy Spirit to make them victorious over sin's power in daily life.

The pages have been written during a busy summer, as I have gone from place to place trying to preach and teach the very truths herein emphasized. If there seems at times to be lack of continuity of thought, I hope the manifest defects of the treatise may not hinder the reader from getting the message I have endeavored to set forth as clearly as possible, under difficult circumstances.

I have not written for literary critics or for theological quibblers, but for earnest people who desire to know the will of God and to do it. And so I send forth this book, in dependence on Him who has said, "Cast thy bread upon the waters: and thou shalt find it after many days." If He be pleased to use it to arouse some at least to a deeper sense of the importance of reality in dealing with souls, I shall be grateful.

H. A. IRONSIDE

1
Repentance: What Is It?

More and more it becomes evident that ours is, as Carlyle expressed it, an "age of sham." Unreality and specious pretense abound in all departments of life. In the domestic, commercial, social, and ecclesiastical spheres, hypocrisy is not only openly condoned, but recognized as almost a necessity for advancement and success in attaining recognition among one's fellows.

Nor is this true only where heterodox religious views are held. Orthodoxy has its shallow dogmatists who are ready to battle savagely for sound doctrine, but who manage to ignore sound living with little or no apparent compunction of conscience.

God desires truth in the inward parts. The blessed man is still the one "in whose spirit there is no guile." It is forever true that "He that covereth his sins shall not prosper: but whoso confesseth and forsaketh them shall have mercy." It can never be out of place to proclaim salvation by free, unmerited favor to all who put their trust in the Lord Jesus Christ. But it also needs to be insisted on that the faith that justifies is not a mere intellectual process—not simply crediting certain historical facts or doctrinal statements; but is a faith that springs from a divinely wrought conviction of sin which produces a repentance that is sincere and genuine.

Our Lord's solemn words, "Except ye repent, ye shall all likewise perish," are as important today as when first uttered. No dispensational distinctions, important as these are in understanding and interpreting God's ways with man, can alter this truth.

No one was ever saved in any dispensation except by grace. Neither sacrificial observances, nor ritual service, nor works of law ever had any part in justifying the ungodly. Nor were any sinners ever saved by grace until they repented. Repentance is not opposed to grace; it is the recognition of the need of grace. "They that be whole need not a physician, but they that are sick." "I came not," said our Lord, "to call the righteous, but sinners to repentance."

One great trouble in this shallow age is that we have lost the meaning of words. We bandy them about until one can seldom be certain how terms are being used. Two ministers were passing an open grocery and dairy store where, in three large baskets, eggs were displayed. On one basket was a sign reading, "Fresh eggs, 24 cents a dozen." The second sign read, "Strictly fresh eggs, 29 cents a dozen." A third read, "Guaranteed strictly fresh eggs, 34 cents a dozen." One of the men exclaimed in amazement, "What does that grocer understand 'fresh' to mean?" So it is with many scriptural terms that to our forefathers had an unvarying meaning, but like debased coins, have today lost their values.

Grace is God's unmerited favor to those who have merited the very opposite. Repentance is the sinner's recognition of and acknowledgment of his lost condition and, thus, of his need of grace. Yet there is no lack of professed preachers of grace who, like the antinomians of old, decry the necessity of repentance lest it seem to invalidate the freedom of grace. One might as well object to a man's acknowledging illness when seeking help from a physician on the ground that all he needed was a doctor's prescription.

Shallow preaching that does not grapple with the terrible fact of man's sinfulness and guilt, calling on "all men everywhere to repent," results in shallow conversions; and so we have myriads of glib-tongued professors today who give no evidence of regeneration whatever. Prating of salvation by grace, they manifest no grace in their lives. Loudly declaring they are justified by faith alone, they fail to remember that "faith without works is dead." Justification by works before men is not to be ignored as though it were in contradiction to justification by faith before God. We need to reread James 3 and let its serious message sink deep into our hearts, that it may control our lives. "If I regard iniquity in my heart, the Lord will not hear me." No man can truly believe in Christ who does not first repent. Nor will his repentance end when he has saving faith. The more he knows God as he goes on through the years, the deeper will that repentance become. A Christian said: "I repented before I knew the meaning of the word. I have repented far more since."

Undoubtedly one great reason why some earnest gospel preachers are almost afraid of, and generally ignore, the terms "repent" and "repentance" in their evangelizing is that they fear lest their hearers misunderstand these terms and think of them as implying something meritorious on the part of the sinner. But nothing could be wider of the mark. There is no saving merit in acknowledging my true condition. There is no healing in facing the nature of my illness. And repentance, as we have seen, is just this very thing.

But in order to clarify the subject, it may be well to observe carefully what repentance is not, and then to notice briefly what it is.

First, repentance is not to be confused with *penitence,* though penitence will invariably enter into it. But penitence is simply sorrow for sin. No amount of penitence can fit a man for salvation. On the other hand, the impenitent will never come to God seeking His grace. But godly sorrow, we are told, worketh repentance not to be repented of. There is a sorrow for sin that has no element of piety in it— "the sorrow of the world worketh death." In Peter's penitence, we see the former; in the remorse of Judas, the latter. Nowhere is man exhorted to feel a certain amount of sorrow for his sins in order to come to Christ. When the Spirit of God applies the truth, penitence is the immediate result. This leads on to repentance, but should not be confused with it. This is a divine work in the soul.

Second, *penance* is not repentance. Penance is the effort in some way to atone for wrong done. This, man can never do. Nor does God in His Word lay it down as a condition of salvation that one first seek to make up to either God or his fellows for evil committed. Here the Roman Catholic translation of the Bible perpetrates a glaring deception on those who accept it as almost an inspired version because it bears the *imprimatur* of the great church dignitaries. Wherever the Authorized Version has "repent," the Douay-Rheims translation reads, "Do penance." There is no excuse for such a para-

17

phrase. It is not a translation. It is the substituting of a Romish dogma for the plain command of God. John the Baptist did not cry, 'Do penance, for the kingdom of God is at hand.' Our Lord Jesus did not say, 'Do penance and believe the gospel,' and, 'Except ye do penance ye shall all likewise perish.' The Apostle Peter did not tell the anxious multitude at Pentecost to 'Do penance and be converted.' Paul did not announce to the men at Athens that 'God commandeth all men everywhere to do penance' in view of a coming judgment day. No respectable Greek scholar would think of so translating the original in these and many other instances.

On the contrary, the call was to *repent;* and between repenting and doing penance there is a vast difference. Even so, we would not forget that he who truly repents will surely seek to make right any wrong he has done to his fellows, though he knows that he never can make up for the wrong done to God. But this is where Christ's expiatory work comes in. As the great Trespass Offering, He could say, "Then I restored that which I took not away" (Ps. 69:4). Think not to add penance to this—as though His work were incomplete and something else were needed to satisfy God's infinite justice.

In the third place, let us remember that *reformation* is not repentance, however closely allied to, or springing out of, it. To turn over a new leaf, to attempt to supplant bad habits with good ones, to try to live well instead of evilly, may not be the outcome of repentance at all, and should never be confounded with it. Reformation is merely an outward change. Repentance is a work of God in the soul.

Recently it was the writer's privilege to broadcast a gospel message from a large Cleveland station. While waiting in the studio for the appointed time, an advertiser's voice was heard through the loudspeaker, announcing: "If you need anything in watch repairing go to..." mentioning the firm. One of the employees looked up and exclaimed, "I need no watch repairing; what I need is a watch." It furnished me with an excellent text. What the unsaved man needs is not a repairing of his life. He needs a new life altogether, which comes only through a second birth. Reformation is like watch repairing. Repentance is like the recognition of the lack of a watch.

REPENTANCE: WHAT IS IT?

Need I add that repentance is not to be considered synonymous with joining a church, or taking up one's religious duties, as people say. It is not *doing* anything.

What then is repentance? As far as possible, I want to avoid using all abstruse or pedantic terms, for I am writing not simply for scholars. Therefore I wish, so far as possible, to avoid citing Greek or Hebrew words. But here it seems almost necessary to say that it is the Greek word, μετάνοια, *metanoia,* which is translated "repentance" in our English Bibles, and literally means a change of mind. This is not simply the acceptance of new ideas in place of old notions. It implies a complete reversal of one's inward attitude.

How luminously clear this makes the whole question before us! To repent is to change one's attitude toward self, toward sin, toward God, toward Christ. And this is what God commands. John came preaching to publicans and sinners, hopelessly vile and depraved, "Change your attitude, for the kingdom is at hand." To haughty scribes and legalistic Pharisees came the same command, "Change your attitude," and thus they would be ready to receive Him who came in grace to save. To sinners everywhere, the Saviour cried, "Except ye change your attitude, ye shall all likewise perish."

And everywhere the apostles went they called upon men thus to face their sins—to face the question of their helplessness, yet their responsibility to God—to face Christ as the one, all-sufficient Saviour, and thus by trusting Him to obtain remission of sins and justification from all things.

So to face these tremendous facts is to change one's mind completely, so that the pleasure-lover sees and confesses the folly of his empty life; the self-indulgent learns to hate the passions that show the corruption of his nature; the self-righteous sees himself a condemned sinner in the eyes of a holy God; the man who has been hiding from God seeks to find a hiding place in Him; the Christ-rejecter realizes his need of a Redeemer, and believes unto salvation.

Which comes first, repentance or faith? In Scripture we read, "Repent ye, and believe the gospel." Yet we find true believers exhorted to "repent, and do the first works." So intimately are the two

19

related that you cannot have one without the other. The man who believes God, repents; the repentant soul puts his trust in the Lord when the gospel is revealed to him. Theologians may wrangle over this, but the fact is, no man believes the gospel until he has judged himself as a needy sinner before God. And this is repentance.

Perhaps it will help us if we see that it is one thing to believe God as to my sinfulness and need of a Saviour, and it is another thing to trust that Saviour implicitly for my own salvation.

Apart from the first aspect of faith, there can be no true repentance. "He that cometh to God must believe that He is, and that He is the rewarder of them that diligently seek Him." Apart from such repentance there can be no saving faith. Yet the deeper my realization of the grace of God manifested toward me in Christ, the more intense will my repentance become.

It was when Mephibosheth realized the kindness of God as shown by David that he cried out, "What is thy servant, that thou shouldest look upon such a dead dog as I am?" (2 Sam. 9:8). And it is the soul's apprehension of grace which leads to ever lower thoughts of self and higher thoughts of Christ.

> *"Let not conscience make you linger,*
> *Nor of fitness fondly dream,*
> *All the fitness He requireth*
> *Is to feel your need of Him.*
> *This He gives you,*
> *'Tis the Spirit's rising beam."*

The very first evidence of awakening grace is dissatisfaction with one's self and self-effort and a longing for deliverance from chains of sin that have bound the soul. To frankly acknowledge that I am lost and guilty is the prelude to life and peace. It is not a question of a certain depth of grief, but simply the recognition and acknowledgment of need that lead one to turn to Christ for refuge. None can perish who put their trust in Him. His grace superabounds above all our sin, and His expiatory work on the cross is so infinitely precious to God that it fully meets all our uncleanness and guilt.

2
The Book of Repentance

"Ye have heard of the patience of Job, and have seen the end of the Lord; that the Lord is very pitiful, and of tender mercy" (Jas. 5:11).

If asked to give the primary theme of the Book of Job in one word, I should reply, "Repentance." As Genesis is the book of Election, Exodus of Redemption, Leviticus of Sanctification, Numbers of Testing, and Deuteronomy of the Divine Government, so Job, possibly written by the same human author and at about the same time, is distinctively the book of Repentance. I know all will not agree with me as to this. Most, perhaps, will insist that the outstanding theme of this ancient drama is, Why do the godly suffer? or something akin to this. But they mistake the secondary for the primary theme when they so insist. Unquestionably this book was divinely designed to settle for all time the problem of why a loving and all-wise God permits the righteous to endure afflictions such as those from which the wicked are often shielded. But behind all this, there is another and a deeper problem; it is the evil in the hearts of the best of men and the necessity of judging oneself in the light of the holiness of God. This is repentance.

To illustrate this theme in such a way as to make evident to every man the importance and necessity of repentance, God takes up the case of Job, the patriarch of the land of Uz, and gives us in detail an account of the process that led him at last to cry, "I abhor myself and repent in dust and ashes."

How different is God's method from the one we would naturally follow! If I had to write a book on repentance, and I wanted a character to illustrate properly this great subject, I fancy I would select a very different man from Job. If searching through the Scriptures for such an illustration, I might think of David—so highly exalted, so greatly blessed—yet who in a moment of weakness and unwatchfulness fell into so grave a sin and afterwards repented so bitterly. The sobbings of his heartfelt penitence and self-reproach, as breathed out in the divine ear in Psalm 51, is indeed the classical passage on the repentance of a child of God who has failed.

Or I might select Manasseh, the ungodly son of a most pious father, whose horrid vices and unmentionable wickednesses dragged the name of Hezekiah into the dust and brought grave reproach on the honor of the God of Israel. And yet Manasseh was brought at last to repentance, humbled himself, and was eventually saved in answer probably to that dishonored father's prayers offered so long before. What a picture of a truly repentant soul does Manasseh present as he bows low before the throne of God, confessing his manifold transgressions and seeking forgiveness for his scarlet sins.

Or I might turn to the New Testament and endeavor to tell again the story of Saul of Tarsus, blameless in deed outwardly before the Law, but a bitter persecutor of the church until the risen Christ appeared to him, as he fell stunned and blinded by "the glory of that light," on the Damascus Turnpike, crying when convinced of his error, "Lord, what wilt Thou have me to do?" His afterlife proved the sincerity of his repentance and the depth of his contrition.

Or if one turned from the pages of holy writ to those of history and biography, he might cite the repentance of the man of the world as seen in Augustine of Hippo or Francis of Assisi, the genuinely changed profligate, or as in the cases of John Bunyan, Ignatius Loyola, John Newton, or, in our own times, of Jerry McAuley, the river thief. In each of these men, when brought into the presence of God, we have a change of attitude indeed that lasted through life.

But if any or all of these were cited as illustrations of the necessity of repentance, how many there would be to say: 'Yes, we quite realize such men needed to repent. Their sins were many, their wickedness great. It was right and proper for them to repent in the agony of their souls. But I, thank God, am not as they. I have never gone into such depths of sin. I have never manifested such depravity. I have not so far forgotten what is right and proper. I am a just man needing no repentance.' Do you say that none would literally use such language as this? Perhaps not, yet the spirit of it, the inward sense of the words, has often been uttered in my own hearing.

Now, in order that none may so speak, when we turn to this ancient book in our Bibles, we find that God searched the world over, not for the worst man, but for the best, and He tells us his strangely pathetic story and shows how that good man was brought to repentance that thus "every mouth might be stopped," and all the world of men might be brought in guilty before Him. For if a man of Job's character must repent, what shall be said of me, and of you, who come so far behind him in righteousness and integrity and have sinned so deplorably and come so far short of the glory of God? Can you not see the wisdom of Jehovah in selecting such a man to show the need that all men should repent?

Consider the case of Job. A wealthy Oriental sheik, apparently, he lived in the days before the knowledge of God had been lost, though it is evident that idolatry, particularly the worship of the heavenly bodies, already had supplanted in places the older worship. For, be it remembered, paganism is not a step upward in the evolution of religion. It is rather a declension, as Romans 1 shows us. Men turned from the living and true God to these vain idols, and "for this cause God gave them up" to all sorts of unclean practices. But Job had escaped all this. He was perfect in his behavior, upright in all his ways, one who reverenced God and detested iniquity.

In chapters 1 and 2, we get a remarkable revelation of things in the unseen world. Job is the subject of a conversation between God and Satan, the accuser of the brethren who accuses them before God day and night. The Lord challenges Satan, "Hast thou considered my servant Job, that there is none like him in the earth...one that fears God and eschews evil?" Note, Job was all that God said he was—a man of faith, a true child of God. This book gives us, then, not the repentance of a sinner, but the repentance of a saint.

Satan denies the truthfulness of the divine estimate of Job and particularly declares that Job does not love and reverence the Lord for what He is in Himself, but for what Job received at His hand. To prove the contrary, the devil is permitted to wrest from the patriarch all that he possessed. Instead of renouncing God, Job exclaims, "The Lord gave, and the Lord hath taken away; blessed be the name of the Lord." Thus far Satan is defeated, but he is relentless.

On a second occasion, he reiterates his implication that Job does not love God because of what He is, but because he really loves his own life most, and recognizes that he is indebted to God for it. Permission is given Satan to put his corrupting hand on Job's body, filling it with a loathsome disease, so that death is to be preferred to life. In his dire extremity, as he sits mournfully in the ash heap scraping the horrid filth from his open sores with a piece of pottery, when even his wife bids him renounce God, he rises triumphantly above his very great trial, exclaiming, "Shall we receive good at the hand of God, and shall we not receive evil?" He glorifies God in the fires. Satan is defeated. Jehovah has made manifest the fact that this man is loyal to Him and loves Him for Himself alone, and not simply for His gifts. It is a marvelous thing thus to find one to whom God means more than all earthly possessions, yes, than life itself.

Thus the first scene ends with Satan baffled and defeated. In what follows we need to remember that Job knew nothing of what had transpired in the unseen world. Had he done so, he would never have gotten into the deep perplexity that ensued after his friends came with their bitter accusations against his character.

In the next part of the book, God has another object in view altogether. Job was a good man. He was altogether righteous, as God Himself knew and declared. But Job knew it, too—knew it so well that he did not realize the actual corruption of his own heart. And after all, it is what a man *is* by nature that counts, not simply what he does. To repress one's nature is one thing; to be free of inbred sin is quite another. Job had apparently forgotten that he was as sinful in himself as any other, though wonderfully preserved by divine grace. God therefore designed to bring this good man to repentance, to make him realize that his nature was vile, though his life had been so well regulated, so that he might magnify the lovingkindness of the One who had made him His own.

So Job's three friends, all men of importance like himself, came to console him. Each proved true to his own clearly indicated character. Eliphaz of Teman was distinctly the man of experience. An observant student of natural law, he again and again declares, "I have seen." Bildad of Shuah was the typical traditionalist. Ask the fathers, he says; they are wiser than we. They shall teach thee. Zophar of Naamah was the cold, hard legalist who considered that God weighed out calamity in exact proportion to man's sin, and dispensed mercies only according to what a man deserved.

For seven days and nights they encamped around the stricken Job, their grief and his too deep for words. But though they were silent, they thought much. Why had these calamities befallen their friend? Could they be other than punishment for hidden sin? Was it not inconceivable that a good God, a faithful Creator, could allow such affliction to come undeserved? Their accusing eyes uttered silently what their lips at first refused to speak.

Job could not stand those eyes. His soul writhed under their implied suggestions that he was suffering for wickedness hitherto concealed. At last, he "opened his mouth, and cursed his day," and vehemently declared his innocence and besought the sympathy of his friends. Then came the long debate. Again and again they charged him with hypocrisy, with overindulgence toward his children, which had brought their ruin, with hidden sin of a vicious character, which God was dealing with. They begged him to confess his iniquities and thus give God a chance to show him mercy.

Sturdily, honestly, sometimes ironically, Job answered them, denying their accusations, assuring them of his confidence in God, though admitting his perplexity. He even went so far as to declare that, if they were right, then God was unjust in His dealings with him. At last they were silenced when, by his final speech, he met all their accusations and vigorously maintained his own righteousness. In chapters 29, 30, and 31, he used the pronouns "I," "me," "my," and "mine" 189 times. But this was before he saw the Lord.

25

Elihu, a younger man who had listened in silence to the entire debate, accepted Job's challenge for someone to speak on God's behalf. In a masterly address, he showed that affliction may be sent for instruction rather than solely as punishment. He exalted the wisdom of God, who is not obliged to reveal beforehand His reasons for chastening. And he pointed out that the bewildered soul is wise when he asks God—waiting for Him to instruct, rather than attempting to understand His ways through human reasoning.

As he speaks, a thunderstorm startles the friends. Then a great whirlwind moves across the desert, and, as it draws near, the voice of the Lord speaks to the soul of Job with question after question which the wisest of men could not answer. He reproves Job for suggesting unrighteousness in His ways. And as a sense of the divine wisdom and majesty comes over the patriarch's afflicted soul, he exclaims: "Behold, I am vile; what shall I answer Thee? I will lay mine hand upon my mouth. Once have I spoken; but I will not answer: yea, twice; but I will proceed no further" (40:4-5).

But God was not yet through. He speaks again, bringing before Job's soul a sense of His greatness and power, of His glory and omniscience. As Job contemplates it all, he gets a new conception of the holiness and the righteousness of God. His own littleness is accentuated. That God should look at all on sinful men now amazes him. "The end of the Lord" is reached at last, and he cries out: "I have heard of Thee by the hearing of the ear: but now mine eye seeth Thee. Wherefore I abhor myself, and repent in dust and ashes" (42:5-6). The great object of the Lord has been attained. Job changes his mind—his whole attitude—both as to himself and as to God. Humbled to the dust, he condemns himself and glorifies the Lord. This is what God had in view from the beginning. And it is what all must reach in one way or another who are saved by grace.

"That Thou shouldst so delight in me and be the God Thou art,
Is darkness to my intellect, but sunshine to my heart."

Self-judgment is the sure precursor to blessing, and self-judgment is the work of repentance wrought by the Spirit of God.

26

3
John's Baptism of Repentance

The New Testament opens with a call to repentance. The ministry of John the Baptist was pre-eminently devoted to emphasizing its importance. Sent by God in the spirit and power of Elijah to prepare the way of the Lord, he found a self-satisfied, self-righteous nation prating about being the chosen people. Professedly waiting for the promised Messiah, yet they were utterly unready to welcome Him because of their low moral condition.

Like the Tishbite, he appeared suddenly and unannounced, a wilderness preacher, declaring to the abjects of Israel first, and then as others sought him out, to the self-righteous scribes, Pharisees, and Sadducees, the need of heart preparation for the reception of the Kingdom. His message was summed up in the pointed words: "Repent ye: for the kingdom of heaven is at hand." It was a challenge to face their sins and the true state of their hearts in the light of the holiness and righteousness of God. And we are glad to learn that the publicans and sinners hearing him, justified God, and were baptized in recognition of the judgment of self and the need of remission of sins.

For with the preaching was linked the rite of baptism. It was definitely declared to be a baptism of repentance for (or unto) the remission of sins. That is, those who submitted to his baptism were practically saying: 'In this act I declare my change of mind, my new attitude toward myself, my sins, and my God. I own my unworthiness, and I cast myself on the infinite mercy of God, looking to Him for deliverance, counting on Him to forgive my sins and graciously fit me for the reception of the King and a place in the Kingdom of the heavens.'

I do not say that all who were baptized entered into its full meaning, but I do insist that this was its true import. Baptism, of course, did not procure remission of sins. It was simply the acknowledgment of the need of such forgiveness. Those so baptized might be likened to debtors giving their notes in recognition of their indebtedness. When our Lord condescended to be identified with this remnant by Himself undergoing baptism He was, as it were, endorsing their notes, declaring that He was ready to meet all their responsibilities by fulfilling every righteous demand of the throne of God on their behalf. It was more than three years later that He said, "I have a baptism to be baptized with; and how am I straitened [or pained] till it be accomplished." Ah, the notes were fast falling due, and on the cross He must settle in bloody agony for them all.

How much of this John, the forerunner, saw it is not easy to say. But that he did have some insight into the great truth, that Jesus was not only Messiah but Saviour, was evidenced by his words, "Behold the Lamb of God, that taketh away the sin of the world!" His baptism of repentance was with a view to the remission of sins through the offering up of the foreordained Lamb as a propitiatory sacrifice.

To the haughty, self-righteous leaders, John said: "O generation of vipers, who hath warned you to flee from the wrath to come? Bring forth therefore fruits meet for repentance." And then he warned them that natural relationship to Abraham would not save anybody, but spiritual kinship only; for faith alone makes one a child of the faithful patriarch. "Fruits meet for repentance"—that is, the changed life must evidence the changed attitude; otherwise there is no true repentance at all.

And then he declared: "Now also the axe is laid unto the root of the trees: therefore every tree which bringeth not forth good fruit is hewn down, and cast into the fire." How different this to the ameliorative measures advocated by many who should know better! Some modern preaching might be summed up in "the axe is laid to the fruit of the tree." Cut off the bad fruit. Prune the tree. Spray it with a religio-philosophical mixture. Change its environment, if possible. Attempt by ethical culture, by religious education, to make the tree produce good fruit—then all will be well. No need of repentance. No place for a second birth. But in spite of human reasoning, the divine principle remains unchanged. The tree is bad; that is why its fruit is corrupt. No use experimenting and trying to produce good fruit from so unwholesome a plant. Lay the axe to the root. Hew down the bad tree to make way for a new one of the heavenly Father's planting.

Repentance is the recognition, the avowed recognition, of God's estimate of the hopeless character of our hearts till renewed by the Word and Spirit of God. Grapes cannot be gathered from a thorn bush, nor figs from thistles. It is not the fruit that must be dealt with. The tree must be removed. To attempt to improve it is useless. God Himself has given it up. "The heart is deceitful above all things and desperately [literally, incurably] wicked." Therefore the need of a new heart and a new spirit.

It was thus that John prepared the way of the Lord. No matter with whom he dealt, he sought to expose the hidden evil of the heart and the need of self-judgment, which is just the recognition that, "in me, that is, in my flesh, dwelleth no good thing." In order to make this manifest, covetous soldiers were commanded to be content with their wages, tax-gatherers to exact no more than their due. Herod, the King himself—who sought to patronize John, while living in vilest incest and licentiousness—writhed as he heard the stern preacher declare, while he pointed to Herodias, "It is not lawful for thee to have her." A prison cell and later the executioner's sword might silence the tongue of the preacher of repentance, but his words live on forever, rebuking still the self-indulgent, the self-righteous, the covetous, the lustful, to the end of time, who fancy they can in some way bribe an offended God to overlook and condone their iniquity.

John the Baptist has been described as "the last of the prophets," and his ministry was certainly most intimately linked with that of the great prophetic brotherhood of the Old Testament. We have already seen how our Lord identifies him in spirit with Elijah; and to His questioning disciples, who were perplexed regarding the prediction in Malachi of Elijah's return prior to the ushering in of the great and dreadful day of the Lord, the Saviour replies, referring to John, "If ye will receive it, this is Elijah which was for to come." He came to break up the fallow ground that the word of the Kingdom might not be sown among thorns. Thus he was chosen by God as a voice crying in the wilderness to prepare the way of the Lord and make straight in the desert a highway for our God. His was a leveling message. There were hills of pride to come down and valleys of degradation to be filled in by grace in order that the divine program might be expeditiously carried out.

In one sense, his was a unique ministry which can never again be repeated, inasmuch as the same circumstances will never be duplicated. But there is a wider sense in which a similar message is always in order, for man's heart remains unchanged and the King is still seeking those who will acknowledge and bow to His authority. Hence the importance of always insisting on the need of repentance, a state of soul which must always precede blessing.

The words of the holy Virgin, in the Magnificat, have an ever-present application: "He hath put down the mighty from their seats, and exalted them of low degree. He hath filled the hungry with good things; and the rich He hath sent empty away" (Lk. 1:52-53). This is the same leveling doctrine as that proclaimed by John. It is the "no difference" doctrine of the Apostle Paul. Yet how the human heart rebels against it. How men pride themselves on fancied distinctions which God's eye does not discern.

"Must I be saved in the same way as my coachman?" indignantly asked a distinguished lady.

"Madam," was the faithful reply, "you do not need to be saved at all. But if you ever are saved, it will be on exactly the same ground as any other poor sinner."

Years ago, I was amazed to hear an eloquent French evangelist, Paul J. Loizeaux, exclaim, "Oh, how hard it is to find sinners! If only I could find one, I have a marvelous message for him." A moment's thought made his meaning clear. To be a sinner is one thing; to know it is another.

Faithful preaching of man's responsibility will drive this truth home to the conscience. Repentance is the recognition of my sinnership—the acknowledging before God that I am as vile as He has declared me to be in His Holy Word. Until one comes to this place, there is no further word from heaven for any man, except the sentence of doom. This truth does not in the least degree compromise the gospel of grace. It rather prepares the sinner to know "the grace of God in truth" and to rejoice in it, reveling in the marvelous provision God has made to "satisfy the longing soul."

Just as one may be hungry and not realize it because of a cloyed taste, and so fail to heed the dinner call, so one may be dying for lack of God's gracious provision and have no sense of his lost condition, and therefore no appreciation of the message of grace. The call to repentance is designed by God to produce that soul hunger that will make the distressed one come with full appetite to the gospel feast. Until one is thus made conscious of his need, he will turn from the gospel story with indifference and contempt. "The full soul loatheth an honeycomb; but to the hungry soul every bitter thing is sweet."

Too often, the earnest gospel preacher dwells on the hopelessness of obtaining salvation by good works, when addressing men whose works are altogether evil and who have no thought of meriting life eternal, but care only for the things of this godless world. We are warned against casting pearls before swine. Is it not possible even in gospel preaching to do this very thing? We may make it all too simple, so easy that we quite misrepresent the God of all grace, who has in all ages first sought to show men their sinfulness and guilt, and then has offered the remedy to those who confessed to their dread disease.

I am persuaded revival would come to believers and awakening to the lost if there were more faithful preachers of the John the Baptist type, who would cry aloud and spare not, but would solemnly show the people their sins and call upon them in the Name of the Lord to repent, remembering that he who justifies himself must be condemned by God, but he who condemns himself will find complete justification in Christ, who died for his sins and who now is exalted to God's right hand as a Prince and a Saviour, granting repentance and remission of sins to all who receive His testimony.

> *"I am not told to labor*
> *To put away my sin,*
> *So foolish, weak and helpless,*
> *I never could begin.*
> *But, blessed truth, I know it,*
> *Though ruined by the Fall,*
> *Christ for my sin has suffered,*
> *Yes, Christ has done it all."*

It will be seen that repentance is the very opposite of meritorious experience. It is the confession that one is utterly without merit, and if he is ever saved at all, it can only be through the merits of our Lord Jesus Christ, "who gave Himself a ransom for all." Here is firm footing for the soul who realizes that all self-effort is nothing but sinking sand. Christ alone is the Rock of our salvation.

4
Christ's Call to Repent

"The law was given by Moses, but grace and truth came by Jesus Christ." Notice that combination—grace and truth. Men must face facts if they would enjoy grace. Surely there never was a more insistent call to repentance than that put forth by Him of whom it could be said, "Grace is poured into Thy lips."

From the moment He began to preach, His message, like that of His forerunner, John, was, "Repent: for the kingdom of heaven is at hand." There is something intensely solemn in this. God had come down to earth and was speaking in His Son. He came with a heart filled with love and compassion for men, so bruised and ruined by sin; but He had to wait on them; He had to press home to them their sad plight; He had to call on them to acknowledge their guilt and their ungodliness before He could pour into their hearts the balm of His grace. For God must have reality. He refuses to gloss over iniquity. He insists on self-judgment, on a complete right-about-face, a new attitude, before He will reveal a Saviour's love.

With this principle the arrangement of the four Gospels is in perfect harmony. In the Synoptics, the call is to repent. In John, the emphasis is laid on believing. Some have thought that there is inconsistency or contradiction here. But we need to remember that John wrote years after the older Evangelists, and with the definite object in view of showing that Jesus is the Christ, the Son of God, and that, believing, we might have life through His Name. He does not simply travel over ground already well trodden. Rather, he adds to and thus supplements the earlier records, inciting to confidence in the testimony God has given concerning His Son. He does not ignore the ministry of repentance because he stresses the importance of faith. On the contrary, he shows to repentant souls the simplicity of salvation, of receiving eternal life, through trusting in Him who, as the True Light, casts light on every man, thus making manifest humanity's fallen condition and the need of an entire change of attitude toward self and toward God.

To tell a man who has no realization that he is lost that he may be saved by faith in Christ means nothing to him, however true and blessed the fact is in itself. It is like throwing a life preserver to a man who does not realize he is about to be engulfed in a maelstrom. When he sees his danger, he will appreciate the deliverance offered. So when the message of the Synoptics has made a profound impression on the soul of a man, he will be ready for the proclamation of eternal life and forgiveness through faith in Christ alone.

When they came to Jesus and told Him of certain Galileans whose blood Pilate had mingled with their sacrifices as his Roman legions quelled a Jewish uprising, and again when they reported the falling of a tower in Siloam as a result of which many were killed, He solemnly declared: "Think ye that these were sinners above all others? I tell you, nay, but except ye repent ye shall all likewise perish." Whether men are taken away by violence, by accident, or, as we say, by natural death, their doom is the same unless they have turned to God in repentance.

We perhaps think of such occurrences as those referred to, as signal instances of the divine judgment against wickedness. But God's holy eye discerns the sinfulness of every heart and calls on all to take sides with Him against themselves. Until this is done, saving faith is an impossibility. This is not to limit grace. It is to make way for it. Remember, repentance is not a state automatically produced. It is the inwrought work of the Holy Spirit effected by faithful preaching of the Word. But how seldom today do we hear the cry, "Except ye repent."

When our Lord looked on to the day of manifestation, He declared: "The men of Nineveh shall rise in the judgment with this generation, and shall condemn it: for they repented at the preaching of Jonas; and, behold, a greater than Jonas is here." Could He have made it clearer that grace is for the repentant soul, and there can only be judgment without mercy for him who persists in hardening his heart against the Spirit's pleading?

And so, when He upbraided the cities where most of His mighty works were done, He prophesied their doom because they would not repent. Bethsaida, Chorazin, Capernaum are but ruins today because, although the testimony given was of such character that if it had been given to Tyre and Sidon they would have repented in sackcloth and ashes, the people in these cities were unmoved. The stones of these Galilean cities are today crying out of the dust of ages, "Repent ye, and believe the gospel." But how few there are with ears to hear and hearts to understand!

It has often been noticed with wonder by thoroughly orthodox theologians that, whereas many cultured preachers, whose gospel testimony is unimpeachably correct, see few or no converts, some fervent evangelist who does not seem to proclaim nearly so clear a gospel, but who drives home to men and women the truth of their lost condition and vehemently stresses the necessity of repentance, wins souls by the scores or even hundreds. It was so with Sam Jones, with D. L. Moody, with Gypsy Smith, with Billy Sunday, with W. P. Nicholson, with Mel Trotter, and many more. Is not the explanation simply this, that when men truly face their sins in the presence of God, their awakened and alarmed consciences make them quick to respond to the slightest intimation of God's grace to those who seek Him with the whole heart?

This is not to set a premium on ignorance, nor to glorify a half-gospel, for undoubtedly where the full, clear announcement of salvation by faith alone in a crucified, risen, and exalted Christ follows the call to repentance, the converts will be much better established than where they have to grope for years after the truth that sets free from all doubt and confusion of mind. The evangelists cited above all came themselves to a better understanding of grace in their maturity than in their early years. But those years were nevertheless wonderfully fruitful in the turning of many from sin to righteousness and from the power of Satan to God.

And is it not marvelously significant that, in the three Gospels which were first circulated throughout the ancient world, the call goes forth to Jew and Gentile insisting that no unrepentant soul will ever find favor with God? Then, as the Christian testimony was better known, the sweet and precious unfoldings of light, life, and love were given in the Gospel of John. Of course, in the actual testimony of the Lord, the two were always intermingled, for "grace and truth" are never to be separated.

Our Lord was the master soul-winner, and we who would be used by God in winning our fellows to a knowledge of Himself may well learn His ways and copy His methods, as far as human frailty will permit.

How easily He might have declared to the rich young ruler, who came running to Him, asking, "Good Master, what must I do to inherit eternal life?" that there was nothing to do, "only believe and live." Had He done so, it would have been actually true. But He did not say that. Instead He undertook to probe the conscience of the young man by using the stern precepts of the Law, and He put a test upon him that only real faith would have led him to meet. "One thing thou lackest." What was that? The young man had never realized his need of a Saviour. Self-satisfied and self-contained, he honestly prided himself on his goodness.

The test, "Sell what thou hast, and give to the poor," was not putting salvation on the ground of human merit; it was intended to reveal to the young man the hidden evil of his heart and to show him his need of mercy.

To the Samaritan woman, He did not give the living water until He had uncovered her life of sin, so that she exclaimed, "Sir, I perceive that thou art a prophet." This was tantamount to saying, 'I perceive that I am a sinner.' And after she believed in Him as Saviour and Messiah, her own testimony was, "Come, see a Man who told me all things that ever I did: Can this be the Christ?"

Scottish Covenantor, Samuel Rutherford, complained in his day that there were so few professed believers who had ever spent a sick night for sin. And if this was true then, it is doubly true today.

When our Lord answered the complaining legalists who objected that He received sinners and ate with them, He related the threefold parable of Luke 15. There we see the entire Trinity concerned in the salvation of a sinner. The Saviour seeks the lost sheep. The woman with the light, illustrating the Holy Spirit's work, seeks the lost piece of silver. And all heaven rejoices when the lost one repents.

The eager father welcomes back the returning prodigal. But we should not overlook the fact, that it was when the ungrateful youth "came to himself" and took the position of self-judgment because of his wicked folly, and actually turned his face homeward, that the father ran to him, though still a great way off, and fell on his neck and kissed him. He did not wait for his boy to ring the doorbell or knock in fear and anxiety on the gate. But, on the other hand, he did not offer him the kiss of forgiveness while he was down among the swine. He hastened to meet him when, in repentance, he turned homeward with words of confession in his heart.

Does all this becloud grace? Surely not. Rather it magnifies and exalts it. For it is to unworthy sinners who recognize and acknowledge their dire condition that God finds delight in showing undeserved favor.

The weeping harlot in Luke 7, kneeling at the feet of Jesus and washing them with her tears while she dries them with her hair—and a woman's hair is her glory—illustrates, as perhaps nothing else can, the relation of repentance to saving faith. Her tears of contrition manifested the grief of her heart as she mourned over her sins and judged her unclean life in the light of Christ's purity. His words of grace, "Her sins, which are many, are forgiven," no sooner had fallen on her ears than she believed His testimony, and she went away knowing she was clean. True, He had not yet died for her sins, but faith laid hold of Him as the one and only Saviour who had power on earth to forgive sins. Her weeping, her washing of His feet, her humiliation—these had nothing meritorious in them. The merit was all His. He who said to another of like character, "Neither do I condemn thee: go and sin no more," had remitted all her iniquities and won her heart forever.

"It is not thy tears of repentance or prayers,
But the blood that atones for the soul:
On Him, then, who shed it thou mayest at once
Thy weight of iniquities roll."

And so our Lord tells us that "there is joy in heaven over one sinner that repenteth more than over ninety and nine just persons that need no repentance." There, where they know what a soul is really worth, every saint and angel rejoices with the Good Shepherd when a lost sheep is reclaimed from its wanderings.

5
The Ministry of Peter

When the Lord Jesus, in the days of His earthly ministry, sent His disciples to go throughout the land of Israel heralding His word, He evidently commanded them to emphasize the same message that John the Baptist preached and which He Himself proclaimed; for we are told in Mark 6:12 that "they went out, and preached that men should repent."

After His atoning death and glorious resurrection, when He commissioned the eleven to go out into all the world and make known His gospel among all nations, we find Him again stressing the same solemn truth. We read in Luke 24:46 that He "said unto them, Thus it is written, and thus it behoved Christ to suffer, and to rise from the dead the third day: and that repentance and remission of sins should be preached in His name among all nations, beginning at Jerusalem." The rending of the veil had ended the old dispensation; His triumph over death introduced the new one; but the call for men to repent was unrepealed. The gospel of the grace of God did not set this to one side, nor ignore it in the slightest degree. Men must still be called on to change their attitude toward God and the sin question if they would receive forgiveness of sins.

True, forgiveness is by faith, but there can be no faith without repentance, and no repentance without faith. What God hath joined together, let no man put asunder.

We are quite prepared, therefore, when we scan the pages of the book of the Acts, to see the large place given to repentance. Ordinarily we speak of this book as *The Acts of the Apostles*. But a closer examination of its twenty-eight chapters shows us that it is occupied largely with the ministry of two apostles, and those are Peter, one of the Twelve, and Paul, the Apostle to the Gentiles who came in afterwards to complete the Word of God. Very few of the other apostles are even mentioned by name. We may say, then, that in Acts 1-12 we have The Acts of Peter, and in chapters 13-28, The Acts of Paul. I propose at this time to see what place repentance has in the preaching of Peter.

In the great Pentecost chapter, we find Peter as the chief spokesman of the Twelve, Matthias being now numbered with them, addressing the multitudes of Jews and devout men, proselytes of the gate, from every nation under heaven. With marvelous clearness and spiritual power and insight, he links the significant happenings of that day to Joel's prophecy of the outpouring of the promised Holy Spirit in the last days. He does not exactly say that Joel's prophecy was at that time being literally fulfilled, but he explains the power manifested as identical with that predicted by the prophet. "This is that," he declares. That is, this power, this outpouring, this divine manifestation, is the same as that spoken of by Joel.

Then he undertakes to show that, after long years of waiting on the part of Israel, Messiah had appeared in exact accord with the prophecies going beforehand. But the Jews had fulfilled their own Scriptures in rejecting Jesus. "Him, being delivered by the determinate counsel and foreknowledge of God, ye have taken, and by wicked hands have crucified and slain: whom God hath raised up, having loosed the pains of death: because it was not possible that He should be holden of it" (Acts 2:23-24). It was true, God had sent Him into the world to die for sinners, but they were nevertheless terribly guilty who stretched forth their hands against Him and treated Him with such shame and ignominy. They dishonored Him. God had glorified Him and had commissioned them to bear witness that He "hath made that same Jesus, whom ye have crucified, both Lord and Christ" (v. 36).

This declaration brought sharp and pungent conviction. They were "pricked in their heart." As the awfulness of their crime burst upon them, they realized the terrible position in which they stood.

How could they extricate themselves from this? In other words, how could they disassociate themselves from the guilty majority over whom the judgment of God hung like a Damocles sword and might fall in fearful vengeance at any moment? They "said unto Peter and to the rest of the apostles, Men and brethren, what shall we do?" Do not confound this question with that of the Philippian jailer, who asked, "What must I do to be saved?" He was a godless Gentile, suddenly awakened to a sense of his lost condition, and he was eagerly seeking deliverance from that unhappy state.

But these Israelites were men of the covenant. They had looked expectantly for Messiah. Peter showed them that He had come, and gone! The chosen nation of which they formed a part had rejected Him. Because of that, God had set them aside as a people under condemnation. In His righteous government, He was about to visit them with His wrath to the uttermost, as Paul afterwards explained to the Thessalonians. If these awakened men, who fully believed Peter's testimony, were to escape that doom, what was their responsibility? What could they do to dissociate themselves from the crime of the guilty nation?

The answer came clear and plain: "Repent and be baptized every one of you in the name of Jesus Christ for the remission of sins, and ye shall receive the gift of the Holy Ghost. For the promise is unto you, and to your children, and to all that are afar off, even as many as the Lord our God shall call" (Acts 2:38-39). Surely all this is plain and perfectly appropriate, as we might expect, for Peter was a divinely directed messenger. The call to repent was as though he had said, 'Change your attitude! The nation has rejected Jesus; you must receive Him. The nation has crucified Him; you must crown Him. Attest your repentance by baptism in His Name. By doing this, you, so to speak, identify yourself with the Messiah, as your fathers were identified with Moses, confessing him as their leader when baptized in the cloud and in the sea.'

John's baptism was with a view to the remission of sins. So with this. It was not that there was saving merit in baptism. The merit was in the One they confessed. Governmentally, however, they

41

passed out from their place in the nation that rejected Christ by thus identifying themselves with Him. That this was clearly his meaning comes out in the next verse, "With many other words did he testify and exhort, saying, Save yourselves from this untoward generation." They could not save themselves from their sins. Only the blood of Christ could do that. But they could save themselves from the doom hanging over the nation by taking sides, in repentance and faith, with the One the nation refused to accept as the Anointed of the Lord. He had said before He went to the cross, "Your house is left unto you desolate." Those who believed Peter's message were to leave the desolate house and go forth unto Him, bearing His reproach.

Nor was this responsibility and blessing only for those who that day heard the message. It is still the responsibility of every believing Jew in all the world, and in a wider sense of the Gentile, too—of "all that are afar off." In Ephesians, we learn that we who once were "afar off are made nigh by the blood of Christ." The repentant man, whether of Israel or the nations, judges the world and turns from it to the Christ that the world has spurned. In so doing, he finds eternal blessing, though he may suffer now for his confession of the Lord Jesus as His Saviour.

In Acts 3, we have another wonderful scene. After the healing of the lame man who sat at the Beautiful Gate of the Temple, Peter preached to the wondering and excited multitude who thronged Solomon's Porch, telling again the same story of the coming of Messiah, only to be "denied" and "killed." But God had raised this One from the dead, the efficacy of whose Name had given the lame beggar soundness of limbs in the presence of them all. The inspired Apostle went on to declare that, though they had ignorantly done this dreadful thing, there was a city of refuge into which they might flee from the avenger of blood. Dramatically he exclaimed, "Repent ye therefore, and be converted, that your sins may be blotted out, when [or, so that] the times of refreshing shall come from the presence of the Lord; and He shall send Jesus Christ, which before was preached unto you: whom the heavens must receive until the times of restitution of all things, which God hath spoken by the mouth of all His holy prophets since the world began" (Acts 3:19-21).

Observe here, that Peter did not proclaim the eventual salvation of all men, as the Universalists and other teachers would have us believe. There is no absolute universal restoration predicted here. What he did proclaim was the restoration of all things of which the prophets had spoken. Beyond that limit he does not go. This restoration is still future and depends on the repentance of Israel. When they shall turn to the Lord, His saving health shall be known among all nations.

But Peter called on his hearers that day to take the course the nation will take later on, and, in view of the promised return of Messiah, to repent and be converted. It is as though he commanded, 'Change your attitude toward this wondrous Prince of Life. Turn right about face, and take the very opposite ground to that of the representatives of the nation, who in answer to the question, "What then shall I do with Jesus who is called Christ?" had vehemently demanded His death, crying, "Away with Him! Crucify Him! Crucify Him!" By thus turning to, instead of turning from Him, they would receive forgiveness of sins and so be ready to welcome Him on His return in power and glory. This was exactly the attitude taken by a dying Jew in modern times, who was heard to exclaim, "Not Barabbas, but this Man!" He had reversed the sentence of his people.

Throughout the entire ministry of Peter, we see the same dominant note. On every occasion where he is found preaching the Word, he exalts the risen Christ and drives home to the people their great wickedness in spurning the One sent by Jehovah to turn them away from their iniquities. Always, in no uncertain tone, he calls for self-judgment, for the recognition and acknowledgment of their sins, and for personal faith in the Lord Jesus as the only means of deliverance. "This is the stone which was set at nought of you builders, which is become the head of the corner. Neither is there salvation in any other: for there is none other name under heaven given among men, whereby we must be saved" (Acts 4:11-12).

Surely no sane, thoughtful reader of the record can escape the conclusion that repentance, while in no sense meritorious, is nevertheless a prerequisite to saving faith. An unrepentant man can never, in the very nature of things, lay hold of the gospel message in appropriating faith, thus receiving the Lord Jesus as his own personal Saviour.

Why, then, should any preacher of the gospel be hesitant about calling men to repentance today? If it is objected that the grace of God was not yet fully revealed in Peter's ministry, I would remind the objector that in his inspired First Epistle, he tells us distinctly why he wrote it. In verse 12 of chapter 5 he says, "I have written briefly, exhorting, and testifying that this is the true grace of God wherein ye stand." How does this differ from the testimony of Paul in Romans 5:2, "We have access by faith into this grace wherein we stand, and rejoice in hope of the glory of God"?

If others object on the ground that Peter was the Apostle of the circumcision and that there is a distinction to be drawn between the message to the Jew and that to the Gentile, I would point to the fact that, in the house of Cornelius, with a Gentile audience before him, his message is of exactly the same character as when he is preaching to his Jewish brethren after the flesh, except that there is no occasion to call for immediate separation from a nation exposed to judgment, and so the stress is put on the responsibility to believe the gospel. But he proclaims, as before, the story of the anointed Jesus, of His death of shame, of His resurrection by omnipotent power, and of the fact that He is ordained by God to be judge of living and dead. "To Him give all the prophets witness, that through His name whosoever believeth in Him shall receive remission of sins" (Acts 10:43). Undoubtedly, he was addressing a truly repentant group, as Cornelius' attitude clearly attested. And in a moment the gospel finds a place in their hearts. They believe the Word and are baptized by the Holy Spirit into the body of Christ and sealed with the Spirit of adoption as the sons of God.

That this surmise is correct is evidenced from what is said by the brethren in Judea, when Peter later on explains why he went in to uncircumcised Gentiles (11:3), in violation of Jewish prejudices.

When his brethren heard the whole story, "they held their peace, and glorified God, saying, Then hath God also to the Gentiles granted repentance unto life" (v. 18). This explains the readiness of Cornelius and his friends to receive the Word in faith.

Only recently the statement was made by one who should have known better: "Repentance is Jewish. Jews could repent because they were in covenant relation with God and had violated that covenant. But Gentiles have never known such a relationship. They are dead sinners. Therefore they cannot repent until after they are born of God." This is a choice bit of ignorant exposition that would be laughable, were it not so dangerous. The Gentiles to whom Peter preached were granted repentance unto life. They did not receive life that they might repent, but through the preached Word they were led to change their attitude and to believe the gospel. Like other Gentiles, they "turned to God from idols," and through faith in Christ were saved. This confirms what we have seen to be the general teaching of Scripture, that repentance is not a meritorious act or a wrought-up temperamental or emotional experience. It is a new attitude definitely taken toward sin and God which results in a readiness to receive with meekness the engrafted word which is able to save the soul.

It is God who gives repentance unto life, but we may say that repentance comes, like faith itself, by hearing the Word of God. Therefore man is responsible to heed that Word, to face it honestly, and thus allow it to do its own work in the heart and conscience. It is this that brings one to an end of himself and prepares the soul to trust alone in the finished work of Christ and so be saved by free, unmerited grace.

To say that because a sinner, whether Jew or Gentile, is dead toward God, therefore he cannot repent, is to misunderstand the nature of that death. It is a judicial, not an actual, death. The unsaved man is identified with sinning Adam by nature and practice, and so is viewed by God as dead in trespasses and sins. He is spiritually dead, because sin has separated him from God. But actually he is a living, responsible creature to whom God addresses Himself as to a

45

reasoning personality, "Come now, and let us reason together, saith the Lord: though your sins be as scarlet, they shall be as white as snow; though they be red like crimson, they shall be as wool" (Isa. 1:18). An examination of the previous verses will show that these words of grace follow a very definite call to a change of attitude, to the bringing forth of works meet for repentance.

It is not incongruous to call on dead sinners to repent. It is the preacher's duty so to do, and it is man's responsibility to obey.

I recognize the fact that the agelong questions concerning the divine sovereignty and human responsibility are involved in this discussion. But why must anyone attempt to explain that which it is above the capacity of the mind of man to grasp? God has said, "My thoughts are not your thoughts, neither are your ways My ways...As the heavens are higher than the earth, so are My ways higher than your ways, and My thoughts than your thoughts." Scripture clearly teaches that God is sovereign and "worketh all things after the counsel of His own will." It just as plainly shows us that man is a responsible creature, who has the power of choice and is called on by the Lord to exercise that power and to turn to Him. "Turn ye, O, turn ye...for why will ye die?" "Choose ye this day whom ye will serve." "Whosoever will, let him take the water of life freely." To those who refused His testimony, the Saviour sadly said, "Ye *will not* come to Me, that ye might have life."

The truth of God's electing grace does not come into conflict with that of man's responsibility. Mr. Moody used to say in his downright, sensible, matter-of-fact manner, "The elect are the whosoever wills; the non-elect are the whosoever won'ts." What theologian could put it more clearly?

> *"Sovereign grace o'er sin abounding!*
> *Ransomed souls the tidings swell;*
> *'Tis a deep that knows no sounding,*
> *Who its breadth and length can tell?*
> *On its glories*
> *Let my soul forever dwell!"*

46

6
The Ministry of Paul

In reading the Epistles of the great Apostle to the Gentiles, one can hardly help noting his peculiar use of the terms, "my gospel," and "the gospel which I preached." He makes it clear that he did not receive it of men, neither was he taught it by those that were in Christ before him. It came as a distinct revelation from heaven when he received his divinely-given commission to the apostolate. Yet when he went up to Jerusalem to see Peter, and, in brotherly conference, laid before him and others of the Twelve the gospel he preached among the Gentiles, we are told they recognized it as of God, and added nothing to it, but gave to him and to Barnabas the right hand of fellowship, commending them to the grace of God as they continued evangelizing the nations. In fact, a rather definite pact was made, an agreement that Peter should go to the circumcision and Paul to the uncircumcision.

Surely this does not mean, as some have contended, that the gospel of the circumcision differed in subject matter from the gospel of the uncircumcision. To hold this is to ignore Paul's own declaration that there is but one gospel. Was he pronouncing a curse on Peter when he said, "Though we, or an angel from heaven, preach any other gospel unto you than that which we have preached unto you, let him be accursed. As we said before, so say I now again, If any man preach any other gospel unto you than that ye have received, let him be accursed" (Gal. 1:8-9). He knew no other gospel. The mixture of law and grace taught by some in that day, he declared, was a different gospel but not another.

Why then the distinction between Peter's evangel and his own? The difference was in the manner of approach, not in the body of

47

doctrine. He defines his gospel as follows: "Moreover, brethren, I declare unto you the gospel which I preached unto you, which also ye have received, and wherein ye stand; by which also ye are saved, if ye keep in memory what I preached unto you, unless ye have believed in vain. For I delivered unto you first of all that which I also received, how that Christ died for our sins according to the scriptures; and that He was buried, and that He rose again the third day according to the scriptures" (1 Cor. 15:1-4). This is exactly what Peter and the rest proclaimed from the beginning, as we have already seen.

Only recently, I noticed the statement in print that, while repentance was connected with the gospel of the circumcision, it had no place in connection with Paul's gospel of the uncircumcision. This is very strange in the face of Paul's own declarations, which I now propose to examine, for he has told us in no uncertain terms just what position he took on this great subject.

In his own conversion, we see repentance illustrated in the clearest possible way. At one moment, he was a self-righteous, bigoted Pharisee who actually thought that he ought to do many things contrary to the name of Jesus of Nazareth. But in another instant, all this was altered. He heard the challenging voice from Heaven, declaring, "I am Jesus whom thou persecutest." Broken in spirit, and convicted of sin, he cried out, "Lord, what wilt Thou have me to do?" It was the question of a sincerely repentant man whose entire attitude was changed when he realized that, in opposing the gospel of the Nazarene, he was fighting against God. The depth of the work wrought in his soul was manifest in his new life and behavior. Soon we see him preaching the faith that once he sought to destroy. We have no more definite evidence of repentance anywhere in our Bible.

And his own conversion was the model for all others. That which had become so real to him was what he proclaimed to Jew and Gentile alike in all the years of his ministry. It was not that he invariably used the actual terms "repent" or "repentance." Probably it was more often that he did not. But his preaching was of the character that was designed to move his hearers to consider their ways, to face their sins before God, to acknowledge their lost condition, and so to avail themselves in faith of the divinely given remedy.

When he stood on Mars' Hill in Athens, addressing the intelligentsia of the city, he used the very word that we are tracing out. After dwelling on the personality and power of the "unknown God" and man's responsibility to obey His voice, he contrasted the present age with the "times of this ignorance God winked at" by declaring that He "now commandeth all men everywhere to repent: because He hath appointed a day, in the which He will judge the world in righteousness by that Man whom He hath ordained; whereof He hath given assurance unto all men, in that He hath raised Him from the dead" (Acts 17:30-31).

To the Philippian jailer, he gave no such message, for the man's whole attitude evidenced the repentance already produced in his soul. Therefore for him, as for every sinner who confesses his guilt, the word was simply, "Believe on the Lord Jesus Christ, and thou shalt be saved." But these proud, supercilious scoffers of the Areopagus were not ready for the message of pure grace. They needed to realize their true state before God. To them the call came, "Change your minds! Your whole attitude towards these questions is wrong. Repent and heed the voice of God!"

He who would be a wise dealer with souls cannot do better than follow his example. The fallow ground must first be broken up before it is ready for the good seed of the gospel.

The moral order of all this comes out vividly when the same Apostle meets the little group of John's disciples at Ephesus. He shows that John's baptism of repentance was but the prelude to the full-orbed evangel of the new dispensation. And this principle abides everywhere (See Acts 19:1-6).

But more positive witness is yet to be adduced, as to his constant endeavor to bring men to repentance in order that they might be saved. In Acts 20, we read of his calling the elders of Ephesus down to Miletus for a farewell interview. To them he rehearsed the story of his labors among them, and of the general character of his ministry. He says, "I kept back nothing that was profitable unto you, but...have taught you publicly and from house to house, testifying both to the Jews, and also to the Greeks, repentance toward God, and faith toward our Lord Jesus Christ." Imagine anyone declaring in the face of such words that Paul's message had no place for repentance, that the call to repent is for the Jews but not for the Gentiles!

Paul saw nothing incongruous in linking together repentance and faith and in the order given. A new attitude toward God would lead to personal trust in the Saviour He had provided. He who sees himself in the light of God's infinite holiness can never be at peace again until he finds rest in Christ through believing the Gospel. "Being justified by faith, we have peace with God through our Lord Jesus Christ" (Rom. 5:1).

In his masterly defense before King Agrippa, Paul explains how he met the risen Christ and received from Him the commission to go forth as "a minister and a witness," and he tells how the Lord sent him to the nations "to open their eyes, and to turn them from darkness to light, and from the power of Satan unto God, that they may receive forgiveness of sins, and inheritance among them which are sanctified by faith that is in Me" (Acts 26:18).

This is the model for all gospel preachers. Our first business is to open men's eyes—to turn them from darkness to light; for the great majority who need Christ as Saviour, do not realize that need. Wide-awake to the things of this life, bent upon acquiring wealth and fame, avidly seeking after the vain pleasures of the world, men rush heedlessly on, caring nothing for the things of supreme importance. They need an awakening message, that which will arouse and alarm, that they may realize something of their guilt and their danger. Till this has been achieved, the preacher's sweetest gospel proclamation will be a matter of supreme indifference; or at the best the prophet of the Lord will be to them, like Ezekiel of old, "as a lovely song" and as one that plays well on an instrument.

Robert Murray McCheyne expressed well the experience of thousands in his spiritual song:

> *"I once was a stranger to grace and to God,*
> *I knew not my danger, I felt not my load;*
> *Though friends spoke in rapture of Christ on the tree,*
> *Jehovah-Tsidkenu was nothing to me."*

It was only when free grace awoke him to a sense of his real condition that he was eager to avail himself of the righteousness of God in Christ.

Our Apostle tells the Ephesian elders that, in obedience to the heavenly vision, he had ever followed this order. In Acts 26:20, we read that he "showed first unto them of Damascus, and at Jerusalem, and throughout all the coasts of Judea, and then to the Gentiles, that they should repent and turn to God, and do works meet for repentance." Is there not some mistake here? None whatever! Can this be the Apostle of grace who so speaks? Unquestionably. Is he not contradicting the very principles he sets forth in Romans and Ephesians? Not at all. He is simply insisting on the importance of the sick man recognizing and acknowledging the incurable nature of his terrible disease, so far as human help is concerned, in order that he may cast himself in faith on the skill of the Great Physician. This is why, in the Roman letter, he devotes nearly three chapters to the elucidation of man's ruin, before he opens up the truth as to God's remedy. And in Ephesians 2, the order is the same. There is no confusion here. All is perfect harmony.

In fact, the more carefully one studies these two great basic Epistles, the more evident does this become; yet both view the sinner from opposite standpoints, though with no contradiction whatever. In Romans, man is seen as alive in the flesh, a guilty culprit, who is without excuse because sinning against light, and who stands exposed to the righteous judgment of God. Whether ignorant heathen as in chapter 1, cultured philosopher as in chapter 2:1-16, or legal-minded Jew, as in the balance of the second chapter, there is "no difference: for all have sinned, and come short of the glory of God." Nevertheless, God visits man in mercy, lavishing daily evidence of His goodness upon him, all designed to lead to repentance (2:4).

51

But alas, so sordid and sinful is the natural heart that, until awakened by the Spirit of God, neither His goodness, as here, nor His wrath, as in Revelation 16:11, will produce repentance. Therefore the need of "the foolishness of preaching." God's truth proclaimed in the power of the Holy Spirit produces that exercise—if not resisted—which results in repentance. This is why the Apostle dwells so definitely on man's lost condition before opening up the glorious gospel of grace, as in the next part of the Roman Epistle.

In Ephesians, man is viewed as morally and spiritually dead; alive enough to the course of this age, but without one pulse beat toward God. From this death condition, he is quickened together with Christ, and that altogether apart from human merit. But this new life is imparted, as we know, through the Word, and that Word first slays and then makes alive.

Bunyan's pilgrim was not conscious of the load on his back until he began to read in the Book. The more he read, the heavier the burden became, until, in response to his pitiable plea for deliverance, he was directed to the Wicket Gate, which speaks of new birth. Even then he did not find complete deliverance until he beheld the empty cross. Then indeed he could sing:

> *"Blest cross; blest sepulcher;*
> *Blest rather be the Man who*
> *There was put to shame for me."*

To cry, "Believe! believe!" to men who have no sense of need is folly. None plowed deeper than Paul before urging men to decision for Christ. His example may well be imitated by others who are anxious to see souls saved and established in the truth.

In his last letter to Timothy, he warns against false teachers, and exhorts the younger preacher not to waste his time arguing with them, but urges him to proclaim the Word faithfully, counting on God to use that Word to produce a change of attitude in his opponents. Note his exhortation, as recorded in 2 Timothy 2:24-26: "The servant of the Lord must not strive; but be gentle unto all men, apt to teach, patient, in meekness instructing those that oppose themselves; if God peradventure will give them repentance to the acknowledging of the truth; and that they may recover themselves out of the snare of the devil, who are taken captive by him at his will." Again we are reminded that repentance is not a meritorious work, as penance is supposed to be, but is an inward state produced by God's Holy Spirit, and by none else.

Some may object, 'Then you tell men they are commanded to repent, yet you very well know they cannot repent unless God produces that change within which leads them to Himself.' Is this really a valid objection? Is it not equally true of believing? Are not men commanded to "believe the gospel"? Are they not responsible to exercise faith in Christ? Yet we know that salvation in its entirety is of the Lord.

In what sense is this true? "Faith cometh by hearing, and hearing by the word of God." If men refuse to hear the report that He sends to them, they must die in their sins. He has said, "Hear, and your soul shall live." The faithful preaching of the gospel and the emphatic declaration of man's needy condition are designed to produce "repentance toward God, and faith toward our Lord Jesus Christ." If men refuse to heed, if like Israel they "always resist the Holy Ghost," they will be given up to hardness of heart and must be judged accordingly. But if they receive the testimony, it will do its own work in their souls, for life is in the Word.

One thing must not be left unsaid—there is nothing that is more calculated to produce repentance than uplifting Christ and calling on men to behold Him dying for their sins on the shameful tree. For nowhere do we get such an understanding of our guilt as in the light of that cross. One may well exclaim,

> *"O how vile my lost estate,*
> *Since my ransom was so great."*

It was when John Newton "saw One hanging on the tree" for him that his proud, haughty will was subdued and he fell, adoring, at the Saviour's feet. Christ crucified is the power of God and the wisdom of God. The message of the cross will break the hardest heart, if men will but hear it. Sadly, it is possible to listen with the outward ear and never really hear the gospel story at all. And it is possible so to tell that story that Christless men will admire and applaud the preacher while rejecting the message. Therefore the need of constant dependence on God that one may preach "not with enticing words of man's wisdom, but in demonstration of the Spirit and of power," in order that the faith of our hearers "should not stand in the wisdom of men, but in the power of God" (1 Cor. 2:4-5).

One would not decry human eloquence, for we are told that Apollos was an eloquent man and mighty in the Scriptures. But we need to remember that eloquence is not power. It is the man whose lips have been touched with a coal of fire from the altar who is prepared to preach in such a way as to bring men to repentance. Paul actually feared that natural ability might get in the way of the Spirit of God, and so he restrained his inherent powers of persuasion in order that his hearers might trust in God's Word, and not in his personal attractiveness as a public speaker. Like John the Baptist, he could say, "He must increase, but I must decrease."

7
Repentance Not to Be Repented Of

In any discussion of the nature and importance of repentance, it would be a great mistake to overlook the fact that children of God may have as much occasion to repent as anyone else. For we should never forget that, after all, saints are sinners. This may seem to be a strange paradox, but both Scripture and experience attest its truthfulness. The closer a believer walks with God, the more he will realize the incurable corruption of his Adamic nature. New birth is not a change of this nature, nor is sanctification a gradual process whereby this nature is purified. New birth is the impartation of a new nature altogether, and practical sanctification is produced by the indwelling Holy Spirit, through the cleansing power of the Word of God, bringing the whole man into conformity to Christ. By the Spirit's power, in the yielded Christian, the old nature is kept in the place of death.

But, through the infirmity of the flesh, we do fail again and again—in fact, will always fail if we turn the eyes of our heart away from Christ. Hence the need of daily, and constant, self-judgment which, we have seen, is the true meaning of sincere repentance.

Failure, too, may be collective as well as individual, and thus will call for collective repentance. For this reason, God sent His prophets to Israel and Judah to show His people their sins and summon them to national repentance. In the same way, in the New Testament, He calls on churches to repent, when failure and sin have marred their testimony. We shall see this in the letters to the seven assemblies in Asia, as recorded in the Apocalypse, a section of Holy Writ which we will examine in a separate chapter. At the present, I would ask you to consider the case of the church of God in Corinth.

We learn from Paul's first letter to this group of believers that it was a church that came behind in no gift, a church characterized by great activity and zeal, but sadly divided by party spirit. Human leaders were being unduly exalted one against another. Sectarianism was rife. This had not led to actual separations into opposing denominations as today, but in the one assembly there were conflicting schools of thought. Heresies abounded, and Christ was being dishonored.

We are not surprised that there followed, in the wake of all this carnality and worldliness, positive indifference to moral evil which had found a lodging place in the church itself. One man among them, and he in all likelihood a person of some prominence, had flaunted the laws of common decency and had entered into an incestuous relationship with his father's wife, that is, with his stepmother. Thus the grace of God was being turned into lasciviousness. The adulterer's course was condoned and his evil life exonerated on the specious plea of the liberty of the dispensation of grace.

The infection was spreading through the church, like leaven in a lump of dough. Others were being contaminated by this vicious example. Instead of dealing with the matter as a grave offense against the Christian moral code, the Corinthians actually gloried in their tolerance and the evil-doer was permitted to sit unrebuked at the sacred supper of the Lord. It was a condition calling for drastic action, but so blind were the members of Christ's body to the affront thus offered to their Head, that they did not even pray that the wicked man might be taken away from among them.

Are there not many churches today similarly affected? Is it not sadly true that in many places discipline in the house of God is practically unknown? Are not adulterers, drunkards, extortioners, profane persons, and blasphemers permitted to retain membership in Christian churches and to defile the assemblies of saints by partaking of the communion feast unchallenged? Is not this one of the main reasons why it is becoming increasingly difficult to reach the unsaved with the gospel? While it is no valid excuse for any man to offer as a reason for rejecting Christ, yet is it not a fact that these hypocrites are everywhere stumbling blocks in the way of the unregenerate? What need there is of a call to repentance being sounded out in the church, as well as in the world!

In the particular case before us, when news of the unholy condition prevailing in Corinth reached the Apostle Paul, he wrote an indignant letter of protest, calling on them to judge the matter in their local assembly and to purge out the old leaven by putting away from among themselves the wicked person. There probably were intimate friends and others linked with this man who might attempt to shield him, but there must be no temporizing. The evil would not allow delayed action. Something must be done at once to cleanse the church of its leprous state.

When we turn to the second letter, we are relieved to learn that something was done, and done immediately, after receiving the first epistle. The adulterer was excommunicated, but not in any spirit of self-righteousness on the part of his brethren. The whole company, with very few exceptions, bowed before God and acknowledged the sinfulness of their former indifference to the evil, and judged themselves for abetting in any degree the gross violation of decency that they had tolerated so long.

It is heart-moving to read the Apostle's stirring words regarding their action and its result. In chapter 2, he opens up his very soul to them. He shows them how deeply he had been exercised in this matter and how hard he found it to be obliged thus to censure his own children in the faith. He was no cold, legal judge. He wrote as a brokenhearted father whose anxiety was great lest he might wound more deeply where he meant to heal. Hardly had the first letter gone forward until he had such serious misgivings that he almost regretted sending it (2 Cor. 7:8); but he rejoiced to know that they had taken it in a good way and had acted resolutely on it.

The offender had been disciplined, and proving unwilling to end his unholy relationship, had been put out of the fellowship of the local church. Now in the outside place, shunned by his former associates as a veritable moral leper, he had come to his senses. He was literally convulsed with sorrow over his wicked ways, and had manifested sincere repentance, turning from his sinful life and walking again in rectitude before God. Now, writes the Apostle, "Sufficient to such a man is this punishment, which was inflicted of many; so that contrariwise ye ought rather to forgive him, and comfort him, lest perhaps such a one should be swallowed up with overmuch sorrow. Wherefore I beseech you that ye would confirm your love toward him" (2 Cor. 2:6-8). As Christ's representative, he assures them that, if they now see their way clear to forgive their erring brother, they may be certain that he joins as heartily in that forgiveness as before he earnestly demanded his excommunication (2:9-10).

Church discipline should always have in view the restoration of the sinner. It is not simply a question of keeping the good name of the church free from reproach, or of maintaining the honor of the Lord; the real object is the recovery of the one who has gone astray. How often we forget this! We either condone evil by failing to take proper disciplinary measures, or we become so severe and self-righteous that we drive the disciplined one farther away instead of solicitously looking for evidence of his repentance in order that we may restore him to fellowship.

The way in which the Spirit of God worked in the souls of these Corinthians is brought out clearly in chapter 7. Note the Apostle's words, as we read verses 9-12: "Now I rejoice, not that ye were made sorry, but that ye sorrowed to repentance: for ye were made sorry after a godly manner, that ye might receive damage by us in nothing. For godly sorrow worketh repentance to salvation not to be repented of: but the sorrow of the world worketh death. For behold this selfsame thing, that ye sorrowed after a godly sort, what carefulness it wrought in you, yea, what clearing of yourselves, yea, what indignation, yea, what fear, yea, what vehement desire, yea, what zeal, yea, what revenge! In all things ye have approved yourselves to be clear in this matter. Wherefore, though I wrote unto you, I did it not for his cause that had done the wrong, nor for his cause that suffered wrong, but that our care for you in the sight of God might appear unto you."

What an insight all this gives us into the real condition brought about by the reading of Paul's letter. And how it emphasizes the reality of their repentance. In fact, the more we weigh each word and study carefully these strong expressions, the more we will be able to fathom the depths of the self-judgment produced in the hearts and consciences of these early Christians. Theirs was a complete change of attitude as a result of hearing the Word of God and being searched thoroughly by it.

In an earlier chapter, when we were attempting to point out the distinction between penitence and repentance, we referred to 2 Corinthians 7:10. Note it now more particularly. "Godly sorrow," we are told, "worketh repentance to salvation not to be repented of." This is sorrow produced by the Spirit of God, as distinguished from the sorrow of the world which is simply remorse because of the dire consequences resulting from evil ways. It is sorrow according to piety, the penitence that a pious person feels when aware of having grieved the God whom he loves, and whom he desires above all things to please.

Note the terms used to depict this exercise. He tells them they "sorrowed after a godly sort," because they entered into the mind of God in regard to the sin that had so defiled His house. "What carefulness it wrought in you," exclaims Paul. Like the Israelites who searched their houses for every possible bit of leavened bread in order that they might put it away and properly keep the feast of the Lord, so they had looked into this question with most meticulous care, dealing with it in the spirit of men who would have everything now suited to God's holy eye, that fellowship with Him might be renewed.

"Yea, what clearing of yourselves!" Heretofore they had been tacitly condoning the offense, thus linking the Name of the Lord with sin, and permitting that to continue among them which rendered His dwelling place unclean. For the assembly of God is His house, and He has said, "I will be sanctified in them that come nigh Me." He is the Holy and the True, and, if He is to manifest His gracious presence in the midst of His church, it is our responsibility to so behave ourselves as to make Him feel at home among us. Have we not all sinned terribly here, and does not our failure explain why the testimony of the churches generally is so powerless and so little is accomplished in the way of winning the lost to Christ?

"Yea, what indignation!" In Ephesians 4:26, we read, "Be ye angry, and sin not." An old Puritan, commenting on this command, wrote, "I am determined so to be angry as not to sin; therefore to be angry at nothing but sin." The enormity of the sin had so impressed the minds of the Corinthian believers that they looked now with utter detestation and abhorrence on that which previously they had weakly excused, as though, after all, it were a matter of small concern one way or another. Low thoughts of sin come from low thoughts of God's holiness and righteousness. Sin seen in the light of what He is will fill the soul with indignation and horror. Nor will it be indignation against some particular person, but against the sin itself and against ourselves that we should ever have thought lightly of it.

"Yea, what fear!" We are warned against the fear of man that bringeth a snare. On the other hand, the fear of the Lord is to hate evil and every evil way. This reverential, not slavish, fear had laid hold on these saints. "The fear of the Lord is the beginning of wisdom." Hence they now put away folly and iniquity and undertook to clean house, as we say, in order that God might be glorified in their assembly.

"Yea, what vehement desire!" Another translation renders this, "Yes, what intense yearning!" meaning, yearning to do the will of God. Where this is found He will unquestionably make known His mind and guide aright.

"Yea, what zeal!" In this they but imitated Him who could say, "The zeal of Thine house hath eaten Me up." To be zealously affected in a good thing is commendable and pleasing to God, as lethargy in regard to spiritual responsibilities is most offensive in His sight.

"Yea, what revenge!" It was not that they were intent upon wreaking vengeance on the wretched man and his guilty paramour who had brought such dishonor on the Name of the Lord, but they visited upon the offender that retribution which God had commanded by His Apostle, that he should be delivered "unto Satan for the destruction of the flesh, that the spirit may be saved in the day of the Lord Jesus." It was love, not revengefulness, that so dealt with him, for things had come to such a pass that temporizing would only have bolstered him up in his iniquity and would have been the ruin of their Christian fellowship and testimony. Put outside, back as it were into that world that lies in the wicked one, he was in a place where he could realize the dreadful state into which he had fallen. Sifted, like Peter, in Satan's sieve, the chaff would be separated from the wheat and eventually his soul restored.

Thus, in all things they had approved themselves to be clear in this matter. Their repentance was deep and real, and their behavior manifested it. Oh, if similar repentance were but characteristic of our churches today, what might God yet do, in the way of revival and blessing among His own and the awakening of a lost world!

The first step toward such a repentance would be our facing conditions, as they prevail on all sides, in the light of the unerring Word of God. Instead of sitting in judgment on that Word, we should let it judge us. This would in turn produce that godly sorrow which results in repentance not to be repented of. Then would come that revival for which many have been praying, and others debating about, but which cannot be looked for until we "search and try our ways, and turn again to the Lord." We cannot expect blessing so long as He has to say to us, as to Israel of old, "I have written to him the great things of My law, but they were counted as a strange thing" (Hos. 8:12).

In the history of God's people of old, we read of many dark days when the Word was forgotten, the house of the Lord neglected, and idolatry had displaced the worship of Jehovah. But time after time God granted revival to His people. In every instance, this was the effect of a return to His Word, producing individual and national repentance, apart from which there could be no revival. These things were written for our learning. May we have grace given to take the lesson to heart and, wherein we have sinned, to confess and judge our evil ways, and to turn again to the Lord, who "delighteth in mercy," and is waiting to hear the cry of a repentant church.

8
Repentance from Dead Works

In the remarkably difficult passage warning against apostasy in Hebrews 6, there is an expression that may well claim our serious attention. In setting forth the "word of the beginning of Christ" (note the marginal reading), which we are exhorted to leave in order to press on to the full revelation of the gospel, which is denominated "perfection," in contrast to the Law, which made nothing perfect, we find the couplet, "of repentance from dead works, and of faith toward God" (v. 1). Because we are exhorted not to lay again this foundation, we are not to suppose that we are called on to ignore the earlier principles in order to enhance the importance of the new. God's truth has been imparted to man gradually, but no later truth demands the spurning of that which has gone before.

By the term, "the word of the beginning of Christ," I understand the testimony of the Law and the Prophets right on through the ministry of the last of them all, John the Baptist, and the added instruction of our Lord Himself in the days of His flesh. All this constitutes the foundation on which the later revelation rests.

It is noticeable that this foundation is given in three couplets. In addition to the one already mentioned, and which I propose to deal with at some length, we have "a doctrine of baptisms, and of laying on of hands," and in the third place, "of resurrection of the dead, and of eternal judgment." All of these six principles were dealt with in, and formed part of the earlier messages of God to His people Israel and to the world at large.

There is no doctrine of baptisms, or washings, in the Christian system. The reference is to Jewish ceremonial washings which sanctified to the purifying of the flesh. The laying on of hands refers not to ministerial ordination, as some have imagined, but to the laying on of hands upon the sacrificial victims, which identified the offerer with his offering, thus typifying the believer laying hold in faith upon the finished work of our blessed Lord Jesus Christ. This has been beautifully expressed by Isaac Watts when he wrote:

> *"My faith would lay her hand*
> *On that blest head of Thine,*
> *While like a penitent I stand*
> *And there confess my sin."*

The doctrine of the resurrection of the dead and of eternal judgment runs all through Scripture. Paul refers to it as part of the hope of Israel, for which he stood condemned (Acts 24:15). It is almost needless to remind any instructed in Christian truth, that we have an interesting advance on this, however, both in the four Gospels and in Paul's Epistles; for there we learn of resurrection from the dead, the first resurrection unto life, as distinguished from a second resurrection unto judgment.

But now we turn to consider the first pair of doctrines in this double trilogy. Here we note the order as elsewhere in Scripture, repentance first, then faith. We have already seen that Paul preached "repentance toward God, and faith toward our Lord Jesus Christ." This is the full-orbed Christian message. In Hebrews, it is repentance from, not toward, something. From what? From that in which every legalist puts all his confidence—dead works.

In Scripture, we have three kinds of works: good works, evil works, and dead works. Good works are the fruit of the new life, and in our dispensation of the indwelling Holy Spirit. Of all who are unsaved, we read, "There is none that doeth good, no, not one." Disciples of Christ, on the other hand, are exhorted so to walk and speak that men may see their good works and glorify their Father which is in heaven. We are "created in Christ Jesus unto good works, which God hath before ordained that we should walk in them."

Well has the hymnwriter declared:

Repentance from Dead Works

"I would not work my soul to save,
That work my Lord has done;
But I would work like any slave
For love of God's dear Son."

Good works are life works—inwrought by the Lord Himself, who works in us—both the willing and the doing of His good pleasure. Evil works are the wicked ways of the unregenerate man. They are but the manifestation in outward behavior of the evil nature that is estranged from God and can only bring forth bad fruit. The world hated Jesus because He testified of it that its works were evil. He showed the source of all this to be the heart, out of which sin proceeds as foul water from a polluted fountain. Good resolutions, attempted reformation, pious intentions, are alike powerless to change this. The prophet asks: "Can the Ethiopian change his skin, or the leopard his spots? then may ye also do good, that are accustomed to do evil" (Jer. 13:23). The trouble is too deep-seated for human effort to change it. Until the sinner receives a new heart, his works can only be evil continually.

But in our text we read of "dead works." What is meant by this expression, so strange to our ordinary way of speaking? Dead works are law works. They are the vain efforts of the natural man to win God's salvation by obedience to law, whether human or divine. But because the man himself is viewed by God as dead in trespasses and sins, his attempts to produce a righteousness suitable to merit eternal life are likewise looked upon as dead works. When God gave the Law, He proclaimed, "The man which doeth those things shall live by them." But no man was ever found who could keep this holy Law, and the penalty for violation of its precepts was death. "The soul that sinneth, it shall die." This sentence was passed on all men. "Now we know that what things soever the law saith, it saith to them who are under the law: that every mouth may be stopped, and all the world may become guilty before God. Therefore by the deeds of the law there shall no flesh be justified in His sight: for by the law is the knowledge of sin" (Rom. 3:19-20).

This is what God Himself has declared, but few accept it as true. "They being ignorant of God's righteousness, and going about to establish their own righteousness, have not submitted themselves unto the righteousness of God" (Rom. 10:3). This was true of Israel after the flesh. It is just as true of millions of Gentiles, who, ignoring the solemn testimony of God's Word regarding man's utterly lost condition, still persist in trying to work out a righteousness of their own, deceived by the Adversary into believing that they can in some way placate an offended God and put Him in their debt so that they can earn His salvation. Isaiah tells us that "we are all as an unclean thing, and all our righteousnesses are as filthy rags; and we all do fade as a leaf; and our iniquities, like the wind, have taken us away" (Isa. 64:6). It is just this attempt to work out a human, legal righteousness that God's Word calls "dead works."

What then is meant by "repentance from dead works"? It is a complete change of mind, whereby the convicted sinner gives up all thought of being able to propitiate God by effort of his own and acknowledges that he is as bad as the Word has declared him to be. He turns about face. Instead of relying on his own fancied merits, he turns to the Lord for deliverance and seeks for mercy through the Saviour God has provided.

In Old Testament times, the legal code with its attendant forms and ceremonies was given, not as a means of justifying righteousness, but as a test of obedience. It was as true then as now that the righteous requirement of the Law was only fulfilled (and that, of course, only in measure) in those who were already regenerated. God has never had two ways of saving people, but different stewardships, or dispensations, have been committed to His people as standards of living, in the various ages. No one was ever saved by law-keeping or by sacrificial observances. To trust in these things would never avail. Not sacrifices, nor offerings, but a broken and a contrite heart, was acceptable to God. All outward forms or legal efforts, apart from faith, were merely dead works, from which the prophets were constantly calling upon men to repent.

A personal experience may make this clear and help to impress it on the reader's mind. On one occasion, upon being asked to preach in a country church, I dropped into a Bible class conducted by a kindly, earnest man, whose knowledge of Scripture, however, was distressingly limited. In the course of the discussion, he asked the question, "How were people saved before Jesus came into the world to die for our sins and to redeem us to God?" Timidly, a lady replied, "By keeping the law of Moses." "Exactly," said the teacher. "If they kept the commandments, they received eternal life."

No one demurring, I felt impelled to ask, "What, then, do you make of Galatians 3:11, 'But that no man is justified by the law in the sight of God, it is evident: for, the just shall live by faith. And the law is not of faith: but, The man that doeth them shall live in them'? And again in verse 21 of the same chapter, we are told, 'If there had been a law given which could have given life, verily righteousness should have been by the law.' Do not these passages, to which many more might be added, show clearly that one must have divine life before he can do what the Law commands, and that no one was ever justified by keeping it?"

For a moment, the leader seemed confused, then he responded graciously, "I think our visitor is right. We had overlooked these passages. Who else can suggest a way whereby people could be saved before Christ came?" Another ventured to inquire, "Would it not be by animal sacrifices? If they broke the Law, did they not make an atonement for their offense by bringing a sin-offering?" This quite satisfied the teacher. "I think that makes it perfectly plain, does it not?" he declared.

But the visitor had to object again, "What do you understand by the solemn words of Hebrews 10:4, 'For it is not possible that the blood of bulls and of goats should take away sins'?" Candidly he confessed, "That is a difficulty. What, then, would you say, sir?"

In reply, I endeavored to show that in all ages men were saved when they turned to God as repentant sinners and believed His testimony. Of this Abraham is the outstanding example. He believed in the Lord and He counted it unto him for righteousness. And David shows that forgiveness was granted and sin covered when one ac-

67

knowledged his guilt before God and trusted His grace, as set forth in Psalm 32. They were saved as truly as we are, by the atoning work of Christ Jesus, only they looked forward to the cross while we look backward to it. Romans 3:24-26 makes this very plain: "Being justified freely by His grace through the redemption that is in Christ Jesus: whom God hath set forth to be a propitiation through faith in His blood, to declare His righteousness for the remission of sins that are past, through the forbearance of God; to declare, I say, at this time His righteousness: that He might be just, and the justifier of him which believeth in Jesus."

I pointed out what every careful student of Scripture knows, that the expression used in verse 25, "sins that are past," refers not to our past sins prior to our conversion, but to sins committed by believers in past ages, before Christ died to put them away. The clause might be rendered 'to declare His righteousness in the pretermission of sins.' Then in the next verse comes the present application of the work of the cross, "To declare, I say, at this time His righteousness," in justifying ungodly sinners through faith in Jesus.

It was most interesting to see how eagerly that little company drank in the truth and with what joy they seemed to apprehend it.

Dead works, then, are works of the flesh, but works performed with intent to earn God's salvation. Of old it might be the effort to keep implicitly The Ten Commandments and to fulfill all the requirements of the ceremonial law. But if the man himself had no life, his works were all dead and could not be accepted of God. In fact, he needed to repent from such dead works, to recognize the folly of trying to win salvation by deeds of the Law. From all such dead works he needed cleansing, as truly as from his manifold iniquities. And all this has been provided in the cross. In Hebrews 9:13, we read: "For if the blood of bulls and of goats, and the ashes of an heifer sprinkling the unclean, sanctifieth to the purifying of the flesh [Note this, for it was as far as the Law could go. It gave outward cleansing, not inward.]: how much more shall the blood of Christ, who through the eternal Spirit offered Himself without spot to God, purge your conscience from dead works to serve the living God?"

This is the gospel revealed to Saul of Tarsus and which changed him into Paul the Apostle. His "dead works" are enumerated in Philippians 3:4-6: "Though I might also have confidence in the flesh. If any other man thinketh that he hath whereof he might trust in the flesh, I more: circumcised the eighth day, of the stock of Israel, of the tribe of Benjamin, an Hebrew of the Hebrews; as touching the law, a Pharisee; concerning zeal, persecuting the church; touching the righteousness which is in the law, blameless." But from these he repented when he turned from self to Christ, and, casting away all confidence in legal righteousness, he could exclaim: "But what things were gain to me, those I counted loss for Christ. Yea doubtless, and I count all things but loss for the excellency of the knowledge of Christ Jesus my Lord: for Whom I have suffered the loss of all things, and do count them but dung, that I may win Christ, and be found in Him, not having mine own righteousness, which is of the law, but that which is through the faith of Christ, the righteousness which is of God by faith."

When Moody and Sankey were having their stirring evangelistic campaigns in England, Mr. Sankey used the hymn a great deal which is an answer to the question, "What must I do to be saved?"

> *"Nothing either great or small, nothing, sinner, no;*
> *Jesus died and did it all long, long ago.*
>
> *"When He from His lofty throne stooped to do and die,*
> *Everything was fully done; listen to His cry—*
>
> *"'It is finished!' yes, indeed, finished every jot,*
> *Sinner, this is all you need, tell me, is it not?*
>
> *"Till to Jesus' work you cling by a simple faith,*
> *Doing is a deadly thing, doing ends in death.*
>
> *"Cast your deadly doing down, down at Jesus' feet.*
> *Stand in Him, in Him alone, gloriously complete."*

James Anthony Froude, the noted essayist, declared this hymn to be "absolutely immoral." To him, it left no place for ethical behavior in the plan of salvation. But he was wrong. It is when men repent from dead works and put their faith in God, resting in the redemptive work of His blessed Son, that they really begin to live unto Him. Then they manifest in their ways the good works which are the natural result of the impartation of a new nature received when they are born from above and so are made members of that new creation of which the Risen Christ is the Head.

> *"What must I do?" has oft been asked,*
> *Eternal life to gain;*
> *Man anxious seems for any task*
> *If this he may obtain.*
>
> *"But all the doing has been done,*
> *As God has clearly shown,*
> *When by the offering of His Son,*
> *His purpose He made known.*
>
> *"He laid on Him the sinner's guilt*
> *When came the appointed day;*
> *And by that blood on Calvary spilt*
> *Takes all our guilt away."*

Happy is the man who sees the end of all flesh in the cross of Christ, and, giving up all pretension to human merit, turns from dead works of every kind and description and rests solely upon the finished work of Jesus. "It is finished," repeated a dying saint, and then added, "Upon that I hang my eternity."

"Repentance from dead works," then, implies the giving up of all confidence in the flesh, the recognition that I am not able to do one thing to retrieve my fallen estate. As a dead sinner, I cannot do one thing to merit the divine favor. My prayers, my tears, my charity, my religiousness—all count for nothing, so far as earning salvation is concerned. I am lost and need a Saviour. I am sick and need a Physician. I am bankrupt and need a Kinsman-Redeemer. I am dead and need Him who is the Resurrection and the Life. All I need I find in Christ, for whom I count all else but dross.

9
Repentance in the Apocalypse

The book of The Revelation of Jesus Christ fittingly closes the volume of Holy Scripture. It deals with both the present age and the coming era, climaxing all God's ways with man, and bringing before us the eternal issues of the long conflict between good and evil. It is the Lord's last word to mankind until the voice of the returning Saviour is heard from the heavens, calling His redeemed to meet Him in the air, preparatory to taking His great power in order that the kingdoms of the world may become the Kingdom of our God and of His Christ. And, significantly enough, it contains a most urgent summons to repentance. In fact, the call to repent is found seven times in the letters to the seven churches, and four times we are told of men whom God had visited in grace and in judgment who repented not, and thus refused to give Him glory.

Time was when comparatively few Christians paid much attention to the book of Revelation. However, this is no longer so evident. People are now studying the Apocalypse, eagerly seeking to find in it some explanation of the present difficult times and some clear light on the impending future.

Many believe that in the letters to the seven churches God has not only given a message that had a direct, literal application to the assemblies named in John's day, but that there is a hidden, prophetic meaning in them, outlining in a very striking way the state of the church from apostolic days to the end of its testimony on earth. All, however, are not agreed as to this.

But one thing is very evident. In these letters the Lord has given us a diagnosis of every state or condition in which His churches may be found at any time throughout the Christian epoch.

Looked at in this way, we see in Ephesus a thoroughly orthodox church that has failed because it has left the freshness of its first love. Smyrna is a suffering church, true to Christ despite persecution and poverty. Pergamos is a worldly church, yet reasonably sound in doctrine, though tolerating much that is very unsound in practice. In Thyatira, superstition and gross immorality prevail, except among a very small minority who grieve over conditions, but do not seem able to remedy them. Sardis is cold and formal, with very little evidence of divine life, though even in it a few are found whose garments are undefiled. Philadelphia is a true Bible church, where the authority of the Lord is recognized and His name revered. Consequently there is an open door for testimony, and faithfulness is manifested in maintaining the truth of God. Laodicea is lukewarm and latitudinarian. Its members play fast and loose with eternal verities and, while professing to have Christ in their midst, He is actually outside the door.

Now to all of these churches there comes the voice of the Lord, declaring, "I know thy works." Everything is open to His searching gaze. It is noticeable that in each letter the order is the same: First, the Lord presents Himself in some special way suited to the spiritual condition of the church addressed. Second, He gives His own diagnosis of the state of that particular assembly. Third, there is a special exhortation or warning, as needed in each case. Fourth, we have the promise to the overcomer and the summons to hear what has been said. In the first three letters, however, the call to hear precedes the promise. It is the opposite in the last four. That there is a divine reason for this is evident, but it need not detain us at the present time.

In five out of the seven letters, we find the exhortation to repent. Smyrna and Philadelphia are both without rebuke, so there is no such command given to them. Let us note carefully, however, what is said to the other five.

Ephesus is rebuked because of having left her first love. Orthodox to the core, this church seemed to pride itself on its jealousy for fundamentals. But there may be great zeal for doctrinal standards where there is very little manifestation of the love of the Spirit. It is a grievous mistake to suppose that the Lord delights in correct dogma and ignores the lack of love. A cold, hard, censorious devotion to a creed, however correct, will never make up for lack of brotherly kindness and a tender Christ-like spirit. So we get the exhortation, "Remember therefore from whence thou art fallen, and repent, and do the first works; or else I will come unto thee quickly, and will remove thy candlestick out of his place, except thou repent" (2:5). How solemn this is! It is not a question of one who has been a Christian losing his soul, but of a church that once witnessed boldly for Christ now in danger of losing its testimony.

Mere doctrinal correctness is not enough to keep the gospel light brightly burning. It is as the love of God is shed abroad in our hearts by the Holy Spirit that our words count with others. Emerson said once, "What you are speaks so loudly, I cannot hear what you say." And an inconsistent, un-Christlike church will cause the world to turn in scorn from its message. So the Lord calls for repentance. That this is more than a mere change of opinion is evident, for He adds, "and do the first works." He would have them turn from their supercilious self-satisfaction to the love and earnestness of their early days, when He was precious to their souls, and for love of Him they would toil and suffer that others might know Him, too. Surely to many of us today the same call comes, coupled with the warning that unless there is a new attitude, a turning back to the Lord in contrition and confession, He will take away the candlestick, and we shall be useless so far as witnessing for Him in a dark world is concerned.

The condition of the Pergamos church is even worse. There positively evil things were tolerated and unholy alliances formed, which were an affront to the One they professed to serve. Again comes the call to repent. Note the words, "Repent; or else I will come unto thee quickly, and will fight against them with the sword of My mouth" (v. 16). What a solemn alternative! Repent, or I will fight against thee! He cannot tolerate unjudged iniquity in His professed people. He will be sanctified in them that come nigh Him. To boast

73

of salvation by grace while living in sin is detestable to Him. The sword of His mouth is His Word. That Word is positively against all who make a pretense of godliness while walking in unholy ways.

Could anything be more needed today than such a message as this? Is not the church in many places dwelling comfortably on Satan's throne, settled down in the world, with no thought of separation to Christ? Balaam of old taught Balak that, if he could break down the wall of separation between his own wicked Moabites and Israel, their own God would have to punish them for their backslidings. The iniquity of Baal-Peor accomplished what Balaam's attempt to curse could not do. How serious it is when the Lord has to take sides, as it were, against His people. But He refuses to condone sin in His saints. Surely we all need to heed the call to repent.

When we turn to consider the Thyatira church, we are confronted with conditions so grave, and wickedness so shocking that we might naturally hesitate to recognize it as a church of God at all. Yet the Lord addresses it as such. It bore His name. It professed to represent Him in the world. Yet it condoned iniquitous practices that were below the level of ordinary decency. On the other hand, this church had once been characterized by love and devotion of an unusually high order, and there were in it still a faithful remnant who mourned over its fallen condition and who were as the salt, preserving it from utter corruption.

Are there not many such churches at the present time? Is it not true that in scores of instances known evil of the vilest kind is tolerated in Christian communities, and no attempt made to cleanse the leprous house? How often have wealth and prominence protected wrongdoers and seemingly made it impossible to deal with them, lest whole families be disgraced or the church be actually disrupted. But desperate diseases require drastic treatment. The voice of God is still calling to repentance. Until there is a changed attitude toward unholy practices there can be no blessing.

In Thyatira there was open immorality, and that of the most revolting type. Like the licentious orgies of the heathen Nature worshippers, it was often practiced under the guise of pretended piety.

74

That wicked princess, Jezebel, who brought her hateful Phoenician idolatry over to Israel and grafted it into the perverted worship of Jehovah, is used as the symbol of what had crept into this church. Degrading and revolting behavior was thus linked with the holy Name of Christ.

It had gone so far, and the proponents of this corruption had been so persistent and so determined, that the Lord says, "I gave her space to repent of her fornication; and she repented not. Behold, I will cast her into a bed, and them that commit adultery with her into great tribulation, except they repent of their deeds" (Rev. 2:21-22). The last words indicate that there was hope still. He had not utterly rejected them. But blessing and restoration were conditioned on repentance. How marvellous is the longsuffering of the grieved and offended Spirit of God! And if today the churches would heed the call, and repent, honestly facing every wicked thing in the light of the Word of God, there would come, we may be sure, revival and renewal that would make the once powerless assemblies a living witness for Christ in the world.

In the church in Sardis we see a very different condition prevailing. There, all is outwardly correct. There is no intimation that vile practices of any kind were being tolerated. But all is cold and formal. It is the respectability of spiritual death. Yet it is evident there was a time when this church was aflame with passionate devotion to Christ. Hence the admonition, "Remember therefore how thou hast received and heard, and hold fast, and repent. If therefore thou shalt not watch, I will come on thee as a thief, and thou shalt not know what hour I will come upon thee" (Rev. 3:3).

One thinks of many churches founded in revival days or reformation times where the light of truth shone brightly and the members were marked by intense zeal and energy. Evangelizing the lost and building up believers were characteristic under a Spirit-filled ministry that made such churches centers of blessing for miles around. But little by little all this has been changed. Formality has taken the place of living power. Coldness has succeeded the old-time spiritual fervor. Academic pulpiteering has displaced the Bible

75

preaching of the olden days. And smug self-complacency now holds sway where once deep concern for the souls of others was manifest.

O that in such former strongholds of evangelicalism and active evangelism there might be a great turning to God, a repentance that would again fill nearly vacant prayer rooms and bring the churches to their knees in brokenness of spirit until God should open the windows of heaven and pour out life-giving showers to revive the barren wastes and give the world to see again a mighty movement of His Holy Spirit.

> *"Revive Thy work, O God,*
> *Disturb this sleep of death.*
> *Quicken the smoldering embers, Lord,*
> *By Thine Almighty breath."*

Such a revival is sorely needed, but it can only come in the wake of sincere repentance.

With the church in Philadelphia the Lord finds no fault. He commends it for its faithfulness and promises rich reward, so we find here, as in the letter to Smyrna, no call to repent.

But it is otherwise with lukewarm Laodicea. Russell Elliot has remarked that "a lukewarm state is not a passing from cold to hot, but from hot to cold" (in *A Last Message*). And this is what has so often taken place. It is a state easy to fall into. Most of us realize that true, spiritual fervor is maintained only where there is a constant sense of our weakness, and the need of much prayer and of nourishing the soul on the Word of God. If private devotion is neglected, we will soon become lukewarm, and the church itself is just what its members make it. These Laodiceans did not seem to know that their condition called for any rebuke. Like Israel in Hosea's day, it could be said, "Gray hairs are here and there upon him, yet he knoweth not." Like Samson, their strength had departed and they wist it not. Backsliding begins so insidiously that one may get far from God in heart and mind before some terrible failure reproves and arouses him. Hence the need of constant watchfulness.

The believer out of fellowship with God may be quite satisfied for a time, boasting of being rich and increased with goods and needing nothing. Yet all the while the Lord detects the sad lack of practically everything that makes for vital godliness. In His grace He sends trial and affliction to draw the wayward heart back to Himself. "As many as I love, I rebuke and chasten: be zealous therefore, and repent" (3:19). No halfway measures will do. There must be positive, earnest endeavor to trace the evil to its source and to take the right attitude toward it and to the One who has been so grievously wronged. He stands outside the door—and note, it is the door of the church, not merely of the individual—knocking and seeking restoration of fellowship. The door is unlatched only by repentance; it can be opened in no other way. So long as there is pride and arrogance, He remains outside. He has said, "To this man will I look, even to him that is poor and of a contrite spirit, and trembleth at my word" (Isa. 66:2). He delights to dwell with those who fear Him and cleave to His truth, but he knows the proud only afar off.

How touchingly He speaks to His disciples, as recorded in John 14:23: "If a man love Me, he will keep My words: and My Father will love him, and We will come unto him, and make Our abode with him." It has often been pointed out that the word translated "abode" here is the same as that translated "mansions" in verse 2. He has gone back to the glory to prepare an abiding place for us. In the meantime, the Father and Son delight to find an abiding place in the hearts of the redeemed while still in this wilderness-world.

Oh, the shame of keeping Him outside the door! Like the bridegroom in the Song, He cries, "Open to me, my sister, my love, my dove, my undefiled: for my head is filled with dew, and my locks with the drops of the night" (Song of Sol. 5:2). But we coldly slumber on, or if barely awakened, find some flimsy excuse for not giving Him admittance.

"Be zealous therefore, and repent." Conditions are worse than we know. Lethargy and drowsiness have blunted our sensibilities. The hour is late. The end of the age draws on. And we are indifferent and lukewarm still. Repentance, if it be worthwhile, must come soon. Otherwise it will be too late, and He will say of us as of Thyatira, "I gave her space to repent…and she repented not."

Oh, what God might yet do with a truly repentant church, aflame with loving devotion to her adorable Lord!

Mr. Billy Sunday, the eccentric evangelist, used to relate a graphic story of a well-known village atheist who was seen running vigorously to a burning church building, intent on joining with others in subduing the flames. A neighbor, observing him, exclaimed facetiously, "This is something new for you! I never saw you going to church before." The atheist replied, "Well, this is the first time I have ever seen a church on fire." Who can tell how many might be drawn to the people of God if they were only on fire for Christ and burning with zeal to win the lost?

> *"O kindle within us a holy desire*
> *Like that which was found in Thy people of old,*
> *Who valued Thy love and whose hearts were on fire,*
> *While they waited in patience Thy face to behold."*

A lukewarm church is a powerless church. There is nothing about it to make unsaved men believe its testimony is worthwhile. But a church characterized by fervent love for Christ, and energetically reaching out after the lost makes an impression even on the most ungodly that it is hard to ignore. When the churches themselves heed the command to repent and get right with God, we may expect to see repentant sinners flocking to their doors.

10
They Repented Not

More than once in the Holy Scriptures we are distinctly told that God speaks to men in the wonders of creation. "The heavens declare the glory of God; and the firmament showeth His handiwork. Day unto day uttereth speech, and night unto night showeth knowledge. There is no speech nor language; their voice is not heard" (Ps. 19:1-3, ARV). Yet nature in itself, beautiful as it is in some things and unspeakably terrible in others, is not sufficient to bring guilty man to repentance. The marvels of the universe ought to convince any thoughtful mind that behind all this amazing machinery is a Creator and a controlling Master Hand, to whom every intelligent being owes allegiance. But something more is needed to subdue the sinner's proud spirit and bend his haughty will to submission, and it is here that the work of the Holy Spirit comes in, acting in power on the conscience of the godless soul.

We have seen that, while the goodness of God was designed to lead man to repentance, yet, experiencing all the benefits of that goodness, men drifted farther and farther along the downward way that leads eventually to everlasting ruin. It is one of the facts hardest to explain that people who are grateful to their fellows for the smallest favors can yet be recipients of God's goodness daily, and that in ten thousand different ways, and still ignore completely the Giver of all good. They forget that "Every good and every perfect gift is from above, and cometh down from the Father of lights, with whom is no variableness, neither shadow of turning."

We need not therefore be surprised that, on the other hand, the judgments of God expressed through what many regard simply as natural calamities also fail, in themselves, to produce repentance,

79

even though they may fill men with fear and anxiety. Our Lord, when predicting conditions that will prevail immediately before His return, describes a world in chaotic upheaval. Nation will be rising against nation, on the earth distress of nations, with perplexity, earthquakes in many places, the sea and the waves roaring, men's hearts failing them for fear—yet no intimation of repentance because of sin and turning to God for deliverance.

It was so before. Amos furnishes us with a striking picture of the dire circumstances that Israel passed through in the days of her apostasy. But the horrors of famine, the loathsome plague, and the destruction wrought by fire, storm, and earthquakes, all alike failed to produce repentance. In this connection, we cannot do better than read carefully a part of his fourth chapter, verses 6-12:

"And I also have given you cleanness of teeth in all your cities, and want of bread in all your places: *yet have ye not returned unto Me,* saith the Lord. And also I have withholden the rain from you, when there were yet three months to the harvest: and I caused it to rain upon one city, and caused it not to rain upon another city: one piece was rained upon, and the piece whereupon it rained not withered. So two or three cities wandered unto one city, to drink water; but they were not satisfied: *yet have ye not returned unto Me,* saith the Lord. I have smitten you with blasting and mildew: when your gardens and your vineyards and your fig trees and your olive trees increased, the palmerworm devoured them: *yet have ye not returned unto Me,* saith the Lord. I have sent among you the pestilence after the manner of Egypt: your young men have I slain with the sword, and have taken away your horses; and I have made the stink of your camps to come up unto your nostrils: *yet have ye not returned unto Me,* saith the Lord. I have overthrown some of you, as God overthrew Sodom and Gomorrah, and ye were as a firebrand plucked out of the burning: *yet have ye not returned unto Me,* saith the Lord. Therefore thus will I do unto thee, O Israel: and because I will do this unto thee, prepare to meet thy God, O Israel."

These sore judgments are similar in character, though not nearly so severe, as those predicted to fall on Christendom in the last days, when transgressions have come to the full. And in that day, just as when in God's longsuffering toward Thyatira, He "gave her space to repent" and she repented not, so, three times over, we find the same thing declared concerning those who shall experience the sorrows of the tribulation era. In Revelation, after we pass the third chapter, we have a series of visions in which is set forth most graphically the climax of the age-long struggle between the forces of evil and those of righteousness. Often has it seemed to the doubting and half-hearted that the victory over sin was never to be won, but that the powers of darkness grew even stronger. But faith could look forward to the triumph of the Lamb and His hosts over the dragon and his deluded followers. In these great visions, the final outcome is clear: "A king shall reign in righteousness." In fact, righteousness shall cover the earth as the waters cover the great deep.

But before that time, there will come the last terrific struggle, when the wrath of God and of the Lamb shall be revealed from heaven, and the wrath of the devil will be manifested on the earth as never before. Ungodly men, caught in the vortex of this dynamic crash of opposing forces, will have to suffer indescribable anguish, if they persist in high-handed opposition to the Kingdom of God. But everything they shall be called on to endure will fail to work repentance in their hearts.

However one may interpret the ninth chapter of the Apocalypse, there can be no question that it is a portent of a condition unspeakably evil which will prevail on earth for a time, inflicting terrible physical and mental suffering on men, and destroying millions of the race. Then note the solemn words of verses 20 and 21: "And the rest of the men which were not killed by these plagues yet repented not of the works of their hands, that they should not worship devils, and idols of gold, and silver, and brass, and stone, and of wood: which neither can see, nor hear, nor walk: neither repented they of their murders, nor of their sorceries, nor of their fornication, nor of their thefts." It is evident that suffering does not necessarily produce repentance. Twice it is so stated in these two verses.

Advocates of the larger hope and Universalists generally insist that all punishment is remedial, and that eventually God will perfect through suffering all who now reject His grace. This passage lends itself to no such delusive dream. Those who are to endure the horrors of the judgments here depicted are not thereby brought to confess their sins and seek divine forgiveness. Instead, they harden themselves against God and persist in their immoral and ungodly behavior.

It cannot be denied that suffering has had a very salutary effect on many people; but this does not refute the position taken above. When the grace of God co-operates with the trying circumstances to bring one to a sense of his personal need, his unworthiness of the divine favor, and his dependence on God for that which alone can enable him to rise above the adverse conditions in which he finds himself, suffering will be used to produce repentance. But where this is not the case, it results in greater hardness of heart, just as the same sun that softens the wax hardens the clay.

A kindred passage to that we have already been considering is Revelation 16:10-11: "And the fifth angel poured out his vial upon the seat of the beast; and his kingdom was full of darkness; and they gnawed their tongues for pain, and blasphemed the God of heaven because of their pains and their sores, and repented not of their deeds." Here we see that the most intense anguish, instead of producing repentance, only hardens men in their sins and in fact leads them to add to the enormity of their guilt by blasphemously blaming God Himself for the distress which their own unholy ways have involved them in.

Again and again we have seen this principle exemplified in actual life. The student of history will recall how in past centuries, when wars, famines, and pestilences have decimated whole nations, the survivors in most cases have become worse rather than better. One thinks of the days of the plague in Paris in the seventeenth and eighteenth centuries, when terror seized the populace, yet there was a turning from, instead of to, God, and the frenzied citizens plunged into all kinds of vile excesses and orgies of infamy in order to help them to forget the ever-present danger.

If a small minority sought after God and recognized that the plague was His voice calling them to repentance, it was only because of His grace working in their hearts. And now that science has demonstrated the possibility of conquering such dire visitations as yellow fever, cholera, and bubonic plague by proper sanitation and extermination of vermin, the majority—instead of gratefully recognizing the Creator's goodness in making known such things to His creatures, that they may protect themselves against disease and physical suffering—actually deride religion and scorn the Word of the Lord, supposing that increased scientific knowledge has made the concept of an intelligent Creator and an overruling Deity unnecessary, if not altogether absurd.

In view of the well-attested saying, that "character tends to permanence," we may readily see what place these considerations should have as we contemplate what the Holy Scriptures reveal concerning the eternal destiny of those who leave this world impenitent and unreconciled to God. We would all like to believe that there is something cleansing in the great change called death, so that eventually all men will attain the beatific vision and become pure and holy, purged from all earth stains and fitted for fellowship with the infinitely righteous One. But the Scriptures positively declare the very opposite. There we learn of two ways to die and two destinies afterwards, according to the state of those who pass from time into eternity. The Lord Jesus Himself has said, "If ye believe not that I am He, ye shall die in your sins" (Jn. 8:24). And in verse 21, He declares, "Whither I go, ye cannot come." In Revelation 14:13, we read: "And I heard a voice from heaven saying unto me, Write, Blessed are the dead which die in the Lord from henceforth: Yea, saith the Spirit, that they may rest from their labors; and their works do follow them."

Observe the vivid contrasts here. Some die in their sins; others die in the Lord. Those who die in their sins never go where Christ is; those who die in the Lord enter into rest and are rewarded for their devotion to their Redeemer. There is no hint that some post-mortem method of purification will be found whereby the first class will be brought to repentance and so to turn to Christ for the salvation they spurned on earth. And those who are in the Lord will never be in danger of apostatizing from the faith and losing at last the knowledge of the divine approval.

The solemn words of the Revelation 22:11, "He that is unjust, let him be unjust still: and he which is filthy, let him be filthy still: and he that is righteous, let him be righteous still: and he that is holy, let him be holy still," make this position doubly sure. Instead of death leading to a continued probation, we find that it rather settles forever the state of the saved and also of the lost. Character remains unchanged thereafter. The righteous continue righteous. The unrighteous continue in their unrighteousness. The holy remain holy for eternity. The unclean are defiled forever. And the reason is that the saved will then be fully conformed to the image of God's Son, our blessed Lord Jesus Christ, while the unsaved will, by their own refusal to heed the message of grace, have become hardened in their sin so that they will be beyond all possibility of repenting.

> *"Sow an act, you reap a habit;*
> *Sow a habit, you reap a character;*
> *Sow a character, you reap a destiny."*

Our Lord's story of the rich man and Lazarus has been treated by some as a parable solely, and by others as all intensely literal; while many see in it a true story in which figurative language is employed in part when describing the unseen world. But however one may take it, the solemn figure of "a great gulf fixed," forever impassible either by those who would go from hell to paradise, or from paradise to hell, remains terribly suggestive. It was surely intended to teach the impossibility that anything the wicked might suffer in another world would lead them to repent of their sins and seek to get right with God. The great lesson the Lord meant to impress on every listener was the importance of repenting here and now, and not indulging the vain hope of some after-death purgatorial cleansing that would accomplish, for the one who died impenitent, what the believer may know on earth when he takes God at His Word. "If they hear not Moses and the prophets, neither will they be persuaded, though one rose from the dead." And if men now spurn the grace of God, trample on the blood of Christ, and do despite to the Holy Spirit, God Himself apparently has no other resources upon which to draw, no other means of bringing hardened sinners to repentance than are now in operation.

This accounts for the few among aged Christ-rejecters who repent before called to give account to God. No one who has worked in government hospitals, prisons, and other public institutions, where he has had to contact large numbers of hoary-headed sinners, can fail to realize how exceedingly difficult it is to deal with them about eternal things. Often my very blood seemed to freeze in my veins as some aged blasphemer has cursed me for my temerity in seeking to tell him of Christ. Never have I heard such torrents of vile words poured forth from human lips as when such have openly expressed their hatred for God and their contempt for all things holy. One could only conclude that years of persistency in sin had hardened the heart and seared the conscience as with a hot iron, so that all desire for anything better had seemingly passed away, reminding one of the awful description of lost souls given in Revelation 18:14, where a literal translation would read, "the fruit season of thy soul's desire has gone from thee."

In the light of these considerations, how earnestly ought we, who know Christ, to seek after the lost and endeavor now, while the day of grace lingers, to bring men to repentance that they might come to a saving knowledge of the Lord Jesus, and in turn be His messengers to others. But if we would do this, we must be wise evangelists, not soothing unrepentant sinners to sleep with a "simple gospel" that has no place in it for showing them their great need, before attempting to present the Remedy.

To Jeremiah, God said, as we noticed earlier, "Break up your fallow ground, sow not among thorns." The plow of God's truth must break up hard hearts if we would hear men crying in anxiety, "What must I do to be saved?" When they see their lost condition, they will be ready to appreciate the salvation provided in grace.

This is what our forefathers in the gospel ministry called "law-preaching." It was the application of the righteous commands of God to the souls of their hearers, in order that "sin by the commandment might become exceeding sinful." We may possibly have a better understanding of "the dispensation of the grace of God" than some of them, but do we get as good results from our so-called "clear gospel sermons" as they did from their sterner preaching? We are apt to be so occupied with the doctrinal presentation of the biblical truth of justification by faith alone that we forget the indifference of the masses to this or any other supernatural message, and so we really fail where we hoped to help. Never be afraid to insist on man's responsibility to glorify God, and to drive home to his conscience the fact of his stupendous failure. Where there is no sense of sin, there will be no appreciation of grace. Do not daub with untempered mortar. Do not be in such a hurry to get to Romans 3:21 that you pass lightly and hastily over the great indictment of the entire human race in the preceding chapters. There is a world of meaning in Mary's words: "He hath filled the hungry with good things; and the rich He hath sent empty away." It is the "poor in spirit" who appreciate the "riches of the glory of His inheritance in the saints."

Our Lord Himself has told us, "They that are whole need not a physician; but they that are sick. I came not to call the righteous, but sinners to repentance." And we may be certain that only a sense of their sinfulness will lead any to avail themselves of the skill of the Great Physician. I have already said that this does not mean that men must pass through a certain amount of soul trouble or feel just so much compunction for sin before they can be saved. But it does mean that men who have sinned with impunity, who have forgotten God, who have scoffed at His grace, or have trusted in a fancied righteousness of their own, should be brought through the Word and Spirit of God to a changed attitude that will make them eager for the salvation so freely offered.

An evangelist had noticed a careless young woman who throughout his preaching had giggled and chattered to an equally thoughtless youth. At the close, an overzealous and most unwise "personal worker" stopped the girl at the door and asked, "Won't you trust in Jesus tonight?" Startled, she replied, "Yes, I will." He directed her to the well-known verse, John 3:16, and read it to her: "For God so loved the world, that He gave His only begotten Son, that whosoever believeth in Him should not perish, but have everlasting life." "Do you believe that?" he inquired. "Sure, I believe it all," was the ready reply. "Then, don't you see, God says you have eternal life?" "O sure, I guess I must have," she answered with nonchalance, and passed out the door. Elated, the young worker hurried to the evangelist with the information that the young woman had "found peace tonight." "Peace!" exclaimed the preacher. "Did she ever find trouble?" It was a good question. Far too many are talked into a false peace by ill-instructed persons who would not know what David meant when he exclaimed, "The pains of hell gat hold upon me: I found trouble and sorrow" (Ps. 116:3). It is the troubled soul who comes to Christ for rest.

How important that such should be urged to immediate decision lest, resisting the Spirit of God as He strives with them, they at last reach the place where they are given up to hardness of heart and "find no place of repentance," though seeking it with tears. It is not that God will refuse to give repentance, but that there comes a time when it is too late to seek to change conditions that have become settled.

11
Does God Ever Repent?

In Jehovah's dealings with the people of Israel, there is perhaps no story more to the point than that of Balak's effort to induce Balaam to curse them when they were encamped on the plains of Moab. The faithless prophet, who loved the wages of unrighteousness, was eager to comply with the wicked king's request, but was hindered each time he attempted to curse the people by the Spirit of God. At last, he confessed his inability to do that for which he had been called to Moab. Instead of cursing Israel he blessed them, foretelling their glorious future in such a way as to stir the ire of Balak, and to move the hearts of God's saints to devout thanksgiving. His narration of the divine purpose concerning the tribes of Israel begins with the remarkable words: "God is not a man, that He should lie; neither the son of man, that He should repent: hath He said, and shall He not do it? or hath He spoken, and shall He not make it good? Behold, I have received commandment to bless: and He hath blessed; and I cannot reverse it" (Num. 23:19-20).

This is a marvelous declaration. It tells us that once God enters into an unconditional covenant with any people, He will never call back His words. And He had definitely confirmed just such a covenant with Abraham. This was before the giving of the Law. The legal covenant they had a part in, and they failed to keep what they had promised. Only a few days later, we read of the terrible sin of Baal-peor. On the ground of law they forfeited everything, and that covenant God Himself abrogated. But His covenant with Abraham was pure grace. He was the only contracting party. Whatever Israel's failures, He could not break His promise. He had bound Himself by an oath and He would not and could not repent, or reverse His decision. His attitude of grace to the promised seed would persist throughout the ages.

How comforting this is to the heart of one who has turned to Him for refuge. He may be assured that "the gifts and calling of God are without repentance" (Rom. 11:29). A careful reading of the dispensational section of Romans (chs. 9, 10, and 11), in which we have God's past, present, and future dealings with Israel, will make this doubly clear. Yet it is singular how many read with blinded minds and fail to get the truth that the Holy Spirit seeks to reveal. Only recently, a tract was mailed to me on the subject of salvation. The writer sought to show that, while in past ages, even in what he called "the Pentecostal dispensation of the early part of the book of the Acts," repentance had a place in the preaching of the gospel as then made known, a very different gospel was revealed to Paul in his later years, in which repentance had no part. And to prove his amazing theory, he quoted as a proof text the words above referred to, "the gifts and calling of God are without repentance."

The interpretation he gave to this verse was that now God gives salvation to believers whom He calls by His grace, on the basis of sovereign mercy alone, and altogether apart from any repentance on their side. Do my readers exclaim, 'What almost unbelievable ignorance'? Yet I have heard others affirm the same thing. It shows how carelessly even good men sometimes read the text of Scripture.

The Apostle's argument is clear. God made certain promises to Abraham. Israel sought those blessings by works of law and failed, so they forfeited everything on that ground. Temporarily, the nation is set aside, and is partially blinded to the true meaning of the very Scriptures in which they glory. Meantime, God is active in grace toward Gentiles, saving all who believe. In the same way, He is now saving individual Jews, though the nation as such is no longer in the place of the covenant. But when Israel shall turn to the Lord, they shall be grafted into their own olive tree again and brought into fulness of blessing. The proof that it must be so is this: When God gives a gift or makes a promise, He will never reverse Himself. He will not change His attitude, for His gifts and callings are without repentance. It is the same as the declaration of Balaam, "He is not a man that He should lie nor the son of man that He should repent."

Then what shall we say of such a Scripture as Genesis 6:5-7, "And God saw that the wickedness of man was great in the earth, and that every imagination of the thoughts of his heart was only evil continually. And it repented the Lord that He had made man on the earth, and it grieved Him at His heart. And the Lord said, I will destroy man, whom I have created, from the face of the earth; both man, and beast, and the creeping thing, and the fowls of the air; for it repenteth Me that I have made them"? Here God is distinctly said to repent, and His attitude toward man is completely changed. In place of longsuffering mercy, He acts in deserved judgment, blotting out the corruption and violence of the antediluvian world by destroying the human race with a flood, except that Noah and his house were saved in the ark. Is there a contradiction here? Do Genesis and Numbers teach opposites? We may be sure they do not.

In the first place, we need to remember that the same human author, Moses, wrote both books. He evidently saw no discrepancy, nothing incongruous or contradictory, in the two statements. And in the second place, back of Moses was God. The human writer spoke as he was moved by the Holy Spirit. Therefore we know there can be no mistake or erroneous conclusion.

Is not the explanation simply this: In Genesis we have a figure of speech in which God is represented as reasoning like a man. This is what theologians call *anthropomorphism,* that is, God, acting in the manner of man. And it has to do, not with a promise made or a covenant of grace given, but with His attitude toward a sinful race. They had plunged into evil of the most repellent nature, so much so that God Himself abhorred them. He changed in His behavior toward them and destroyed them instead of preserving them in their corruption. He has thus dealt with sinful nations and individuals.

But where His pledged word has been given, He never repents. "I am the Lord, I change not; therefore ye sons of Jacob are not consumed." How wondrous the grace that shines out in words such as these! Not all the waywardness of His people can make Him change

His mind, once He has given His promise, or cause Him to alter His attitude toward them when He has entered into covenant with them.

It is because of Christ and His redemptive work that He, the Holy One, can thus bless a sinful nation. And concerning Christ Himself, who has become the Mediator of the New Covenant, He declares: "The Lord hath sworn, and will not repent, Thou art a priest forever after the order of Melchizedek" (Ps. 110:4). Thus has our blessed Lord been confirmed as "a surety of a better testament" than that of legal works. He is the Man of God's purpose, who represents all His people before the throne in heaven, and in whom all the promises of God are "yea and amen."

Our Lord Jesus Christ is the "exact expression of His [that is, God's] character" (Heb. 1:3, literal rendering); therefore we are not surprised to find that there is no such thing as repentance in His attitude toward the Father or toward mankind. Horace Bushnell, in his *Character of Jesus,* drew attention to the essential difference between His piety and that of all others who profess His Name. We are sinners, and we must come to God as such if we would ever be saved at all. Therefore, we come to Him confessing our iniquities and bowing before Him in repentance. It was thus the publican in the parable came. "God," he exclaimed, "be propitious to me the sinner." Propitiation was made on the cross. But our attitude of soul must still be the same as his. We come confessing we are without merit and trusting in Him who is the propitiation for our sins. Until we take this position before God, we cannot really know Him as Father, and so enter into fellowship with Him.

But the piety of Jesus was on a totally different basis. He never confessed a sin either against God or man, in thought, word, or deed. He taught others to pray, "Forgive us our debts, as we forgive our debtors." But He could never join with them in the use of such words. In fact, nothing brings out more clearly the essential difference between Him and us than the amazing fact that He is never found praying with anyone. Some of our most blessed experiences are enjoyed as we bow reverently before God with fellow believers, together acknowledging our mutual needs and confessing our common sins. But He never had such experiences. He prayed for others, not with them, because His relationship was different from ours. He was "the only begotten of the Father, full of grace and truth." He prayed as the Son in manhood, who was nevertheless ever dwelling in the bosom of the Father. Hence He never shed one tear over His own sins or shortcomings, for He had none. He wept for those of others, but never for His own. His was "piety without one dash of repentance," to quote Bushnell again. He never sought for forgiveness. For He was ever the unblemished, spotless Lamb of God, perfect without and within, who came into the world to offer Himself without spot to God for our redemption.

If any have not yet sensed the vast chasm separating His holy humanity from our poor, fallen, sinful nature, let them weigh these things carefully. "If we say that we have no sin, we deceive ourselves, and the truth is not in us" (1 Jn. 1:8). But He definitely challenged His bitterest foes to give evidence that He had come short in anything. "Which of you convinceth me of sin?" To this day, none have ever been able to reply to this challenge by pointing out one flaw in His life, one defect in His character, or one error in His judgment. He never retracted anything. He never said, "I am sorry." He never apologized for any offense committed. He could say, "I do always those things that please Him." And it was this very perfection of His character that fitted Him to make expiation for our guilt. God "hath made Him to be sin for us, who knew no sin; that we might be made the righteousness of God in Him" (2 Cor. 5:21).

It is true that, as Captain of our salvation, He was perfected through sufferings (Heb. 2:10). As to His nature, He was perfect throughout. From babyhood to His death upon the cross, He was the Holy One. But if He would become our Redeemer, He must win the title by His sufferings. Only in this sense could He be said to be perfected. He who had always commanded, deigned to take the servant's form and "to learn obedience" as He walked this scene in holy subjection to the Father's will. "I came," He said, "not to do Mine own will, but the will of Him that sent Me." And such delight did the Father have in this perfect devotion of Jesus that He twice opened the heavens to declare, "This is My beloved Son, in whom I am well pleased; hear ye Him."

Surely the more we contemplate with adoring love His matchless perfections, the lower we will bow in humiliation before Him, confessing our sins and repenting, like Job, in sackcloth and ashes. It was the revelation of the wisdom and majesty of God that brought the patriarch of old to that place. How much more may we be humbled as we behold His love and holiness meeting in Christ. In Him, "Mercy and truth have met together; righteousness and peace have kissed each other." His cross reveals, as nothing else could, our sinfulness and His holy love. If God has so loved us as to give His Son to put away sin by the sacrifice of Himself, how can we ever doubt His intention to save eternally all who bow in repentance before Him and put in their plea as sinners, trusting His matchless grace?

Having "spared not His own Son, but delivered Him up for us all, how shall He not with Him also freely give us all things?" He knew all we were, and all we would ever be, when He put us in Christ. Nothing now will ever cause Him to repent or to change His attitude toward us. It is not humility to doubt Him, and to wonder whether He will really bring us through to heaven at last. On the contrary, it is downright unbelief. "Hath He spoken, and shall He not do it?" Faith sets its seal to what God has said and rests serenely on that inviolable pledge, knowing that "God is not a man, that He should lie, neither the son of man, that He should repent."

It is true; He will not be indifferent to our sins as believers. "Whom the Lord loveth He chasteneth, and scourgeth every son whom He receiveth." "As many as I love, I rebuke and chasten: be zealous therefore, and repent." But He will never cast us off, however severely He may have to chastise us if we persist in wilfully disobeying His Word.

The principle on which He deals with erring believers is clearly set forth in Psalm 89:27-36: "Also I will make Him my firstborn, higher than the kings of the earth. My mercy will I keep for him for evermore, and My covenant shall stand fast with him. His seed also will I make to endure forever, and his throne as the days of heaven.

Does God Ever Repent?

If his children forsake My law, and walk not in My judgments; if they break My statutes, and keep not My commandments; then will I visit their transgression with the rod, and their iniquity with stripes. Nevertheless My lovingkindness will I not utterly take from him, nor suffer My faithfulness to fail. My covenant will I not break, nor alter the thing that is gone out of My lips. Once have I sworn by My holiness, that I will not lie unto David. His seed shall endure forever, and his throne as the sun before Me."

He has promised His Son to take to glory all who put their trust in Him. He will discipline them if wayward; but He will never cast them off, for the blood of the cross has settled the sin question eternally for all who believe.

Listen to Paul's exultant words (Rom. 8:38-39): "For I am persuaded that neither death, nor life, nor angels, nor principalities, nor powers, nor things present, nor things to come, nor height, nor depth, nor any other creature, shall be able to separate us from the love of God, which is in Christ Jesus our Lord." What is there that is neither a thing present, nor a thing to come? What is there that is included neither in life nor in death? Could stronger words be used to assure us that God will never repent of His purpose in Christ?

What we need to see, then, is that He who created man might well repent that He had made him when He saw the depth of wickedness into which the race had fallen, and so He determined to blot them out in the judgment of the flood, as later on His patience came to an end with the corrupt inhabitants of Sodom and Gomorrah and the cities of the plain after He had (to use another biblical anthropomorphism) come down to see if they were as bad as had been reported. He gave Canaan to seven great and powerful nations, but when at last the iniquity of the Amorites was full, He used the armies of Israel to destroy them. As Moral Governor of the universe, He has used one nation to chastise another, and then in turn punished the people thus used, when they too became as vile as, or worse than, those they had destroyed. In all such instances, it may be said that "it repented the Lord that He had made man," or permitted certain blessings to be lavished on him. But when He gives His

95

pledged word to deliver and to bless, He never repents. His promises are irrevocable, based on what He is, not on what man deserves.

In the stirring little book of Hosea, God is portrayed as still yearning over Israel, even after He has decreed their judgment. Likening them to the cities of the plain, destroyed with Sodom, He cries, "How shall I give thee up, Ephraim? how shall I deliver thee, Israel? how shall I make thee as Admah? how shall I set thee as Zeboim? Mine heart is turned within Me, My repentings are kindled together. I will not execute the fierceness of Mine anger, I will not return to destroy Ephraim: for I am God, and not man; the Holy One in the midst of thee: and I will not enter into the city" (Hos. 11:8-9). This is most heart-moving. He who will never repent when He promises blessing is pictured as repenting concerning the predicted doom of His people. He would, as it were, alter His attitude toward them if they would but change theirs toward Him. It is enough to stir the soul to its depths. Yet on Israel's part there was no response, and judgment had to take its course.

But the future holds promise of a glorious recovery. All, even of the rejected nation, who have personally sought His face in blessing will have part in resurrection glory. So God gives the gracious assurance of Hosea 13:14: "I will ransom them from the power of the grave; I will redeem them from death: O death, I will be thy plagues; O grave, I will be thy destruction: repentance shall be hid from Mine eyes." Nothing shall ever take place in all the ages to come that will invalidate or alter His settled purpose of grace. He will never, by any possibility, change His attitude toward those whom He has redeemed to Himself.

> *"His is an unchanging love,*
> *Higher than the heights above,*
> *Deeper than the depths beneath,*
> *True and faithful, strong as death."*

12
Impossible to Renew to Repentance

In Peter's second letter, I believe he identifies for us the author, under God, of the Epistle to the Hebrews. He mentions a letter written to Jewish believers by "our beloved brother Paul," "in which are some things hard to be understood, which they that are unlearned and unstable wrest...unto their own destruction" (2 Pet. 3:15-16). As we know, Peter's special ministry was to the circumcision, and he addresses his letters to Christian Jews of the Diaspora, that is, those dispersed among the Gentiles. The letter to the Hebrews therefore must be that referred to in the verses quoted, as no other of Paul's Epistles is addressed to Hebrew believers. And surely there is no other letter in the New Testament which contains more difficult statements than this one.

How frequently have ignorant and poorly instructed saints misunderstood such passages as the first part of chapter 6 and the last half of chapter 10. Terrified by what was only intended as a warning against apostasy, true lovers of Christ have fancied that they have committed the unpardonable sin and, by crucifying the Son of God afresh, have put themselves beyond the pale of mercy. Reason has tottered on the throne as the terrible thought has gripped their consciousness that for them there is now no hope, for so grave is their sin, they fear, it is impossible "to renew them again unto repentance."

Various explanations, or attempted explanations, have been given of the passages in question, and godly men have differed greatly as to their proper application. Without going into the subject extensively, it nevertheless seems desirable that we should, in this connection, try to get a real understanding of what is involved in both these solemn warnings. Note carefully the exact words of Hebrews 6:1-13. The paragraph is somewhat lengthy, but it seems necessary to have it all in view if we are to grasp its import properly.

"Therefore, leaving the principles of the doctrine of Christ, let us go on unto perfection; not laying again the foundation of repentance from dead works, and of faith toward God, of the doctrine of baptisms, and of laying on of hands, and of resurrection of the dead, and of eternal judgment. And this will we do, if God permit.

"For it is impossible for those who were once enlightened, and have tasted of the heavenly gift, and were made partakers of the Holy Ghost, and have tasted the good word of God, and the powers of the world to come, if they shall fall away, to renew them again unto repentance; seeing they crucify to themselves the Son of God afresh, and put Him to an open shame.

"For the earth which drinketh in the rain that cometh oft upon it, and bringeth forth herbs meet for them by whom it is dressed, receiveth blessing from God: but that which beareth thorns and briers is rejected, and is nigh unto cursing; whose end is to be burned.

"But, beloved, we are persuaded better things of you, and things that accompany salvation, though we thus speak. For God is not unrighteous to forget your work and labor of love, which ye have showed toward His name, in that ye have ministered to the saints, and do minister. And we desire that every one of you do show the same diligence to the full assurance of hope unto the end: that ye be not slothful, but followers of them who through faith and patience inherit the promises. For when God made promise to Abraham, because He could swear by no greater, He sware by Himself."

In a previous chapter, we have already glanced at verses 1-3. There we saw that "the first principles of the doctrine of Christ," or as the marginal rendering reads, "the word of the beginning of Christ," refers to the preparatory or foundation teaching of the former dispensation, apart from which it is next to impossible really to understand the true Christian doctrine. "Perfection" as used here has no reference to experience, but rather to the body of New Testament teaching which, for the well-instructed believer, supersedes the foundation teaching of that past age. The tendency of these converted Hebrews, or of those among them who professed to be converted through the gospel message, was to look back longingly to the ritual practices and the partial revelation of the Old Testament, in place of going on to a full understanding and appreciation of the present truth. The Epistle is throughout a warning against possible apostasy where there was unreality, and an exhortation to "go on" to the better things of the New Covenant as contrasted with the lesser things of the Old.

Before examining the solemn statements of verses 4-6, let us consider the closing part of this section, verses 9-13. The writer of Hebrews has no question concerning the ultimate fate of those truly saved, though he warns them of the danger involved in spiritual sloth and indifference. But after setting forth the hopeless condition of the apostates depicted in verses 4-8, he says, "But, beloved, we are persuaded better things of you, and things that accompany salvation, though we thus speak."

This is most important. If these words mean anything at all, they surely tell us that people might pass through all that is mentioned in verses 4 and 5 without being saved at all. Note this carefully; it will save from confusion of mind: Whatever else the five statements that are enumerated in these verses mean, they do not necessarily accompany salvation. All of them might be true, and yet the soul remain out of Christ.

The evidences of divine life are given in the following verses. There was real devotion to the Lord Himself and unselfish care for His suffering people, seen in these converted Hebrews. Not merely the acceptance of certain doctrines, however true, but real trust in a living Saviour, had made them new creatures, and so their outward walk evidenced the inward change that had taken place. God, the righteous One, would not overlook all this in the day when He would have to judge the nation to which these believers belonged by natural birth. He would not leave a doubt in the minds of any who truly rested in Christ as to the genuineness of their conversion, even when He warned of the possibility of any unreal professors who had gotten in among them eventually apostatizing. But he would have all carefully examine the foundations of their hope of salvation.

If this is clear now go back and read again the warning: "For it is impossible for those who were once enlightened, and have tasted of the heavenly gift, and were made partakers of the Holy Ghost, and have tasted the good word of God, and the powers of the world to come, if they shall fall away, to renew them again unto repentance; seeing they crucify to themselves the Son of God afresh, and put Him to an open shame." Who were the people here contemplated? According to verse 9 they were not saved people. In other words, they had never been born again of the Word and Spirit of God.

Who, then, were they? The answer is plain. They were professed converts to Christianity who had witnessed much of the supernatural character of the new and gracious movement, but they had never actually known Christ. They were like those in our Lord's day who believed in the miracles, but did not know the One who wrought them. What is said of their past? There are five statements.

First, they had been enlightened. This is true of every one who listens thoughtfully to the preaching of the gospel. Light is thereby imparted to him to which he was a stranger before. "The entrance of Thy words giveth light; it giveth understanding unto the simple." But unhappily many have been thus enlightened who refuse to walk in the light.

We learn in 1 John 1:7 that, "If we walk in the light, as He is in the light, we have fellowship one with another, and the blood of Jesus Christ His Son cleanseth us from all sin." Notice it is where you walk, not how. "Ye were sometimes darkness, but now are ye light in the Lord." The man who walks in the light, the revealing power of God's truth, does not shun its manifestations or turn from its fierce revealing blaze. "God is light, and in Him is no darkness at all." Facing the light, walking in it, he learns that the blood is sprinkled on the mercy seat from which the light shines. He no longer dreads its brightness but allows it to search him to the depths of his being, knowing that the blood meets every evil thing that is thus exposed. This is a very different thing from being simply enlightened.

In the second place, they had tasted of the heavenly gift. Now whether we think of this gift being the Lord Jesus Himself, whom God the Father gave to be the propitiation for our sins, or whether we think of it as that eternal life which is definitely called "the gift of God," it is quite evident that there are many who are, for a time, greatly impressed by the amazing fact that God has so loved the world as to send His Son into the world that He might give eternal life to all who trust Him; and yet they never truly feed on the Living Bread that came down from heaven to give life to all who believe on His Name. To taste is one thing; to eat is quite another. There are vast numbers of persons who once seemed to appreciate Christ, but have since proven that they never really knew Him, whom to know is life eternal.

Third, they "were made partakers of the Holy Spirit." Surely this implies reality. How could anyone be a partaker of the Spirit of God, and not be saved?

I answer, Balaam was; and so was Judas. Yet both are lost. The Spirit of God is sovereign in His working. Yet He compels no one to surrender to Christ, though none would do so apart from His gracious brooding over their hearts. But men may experience much of His convicting power and be deeply stirred as He portrays the preciousness of Christ, and yet may resist His wooing and refuse to heed His message.

Note carefully we are not told that those apostates had ever been regenerated by the Spirit, or sealed, or anointed, or baptized, or filled. They simply became partakers of His power; but did not go on to know truly the Lord. Balaam is a sad example of this, he who felt the power of the Spirit upon him, but "loved the wages of unrighteousness" and never repented of his base intentions, even though not permitted to carry them out. Did not Judas work miracles with the rest in the energy of the Spirit? Apparently he did, for all the Twelve told how the demons were subject unto them, but our Lord declared he was a devil; and we are told he died a suicide and went to his own place.

Fourth, they "tasted the good Word of God." This is closely allied to the first statement made by the inspired writer concerning them, yet it is not exactly repetition. They heard the Word preached. It appealed to them. They felt it to be what they needed. But, though they tasted its preciousness, they did not feed on it with a living faith.

And lastly, they had known something of the "powers of the world [or age] to come." The reference is to the miraculous signs that were given by the Lord to authenticate the early Christian message. In the coming age, miracles will be the ordinary thing. At the beginning of this dispensation of grace, they were given by our merciful God in order that men might be without excuse for rejecting His Word. And these Hebrews had seen many signs and wonders, so that they were, for a time at least, intellectually convinced of the truth of the new doctrine. But that truth had not been received into the heart. They knew much about Jesus, the Prophet, mighty in word and deed, but they did not know Him as Saviour and Lord by yielding themselves to His authority. While our Lord was on earth, there were numbers of temporary followers who believed on Him when they saw the miracles that He wrought, but afterwards went back and walked no more with Him. Continuance is a proof of reality.

We may well challenge our own hearts as to whether we are in any better case than they. Formalists and hypocrites abound on every hand. If we profess to trust Him, do we love Him and seek to glorify Him in our lives? An empty profession saves no one.

In the hour of testing, these Hebrews turned back to Judaism. Apparently they were not prepared for the suffering that Christians were called upon to pass through for the Name of the Lord Jesus. So they turned their backs on Christianity and relapsed into Judaism. In so doing, they rejected every testimony that even God could give them. He had nothing hidden in reserve. He had told out all His heart when He spoke in His Son. For those who deliberately and definitely refused to accept that testimony, God had nothing more to say. It was impossible to renew them again unto repentance. They

positively and defiantly sided with His murderers, and so they crucified the Son of God afresh and put Him to an open shame.

We are not told that God would refuse to save them if at the last
they acknowledged their guilt, bad as it was, and sought His forgiveness. We are told that they had so sinned against all light and all
knowledge that God had nothing further to put before them. The
Spirit of God had given them up, and the day for repentance had
gone by. It was not that He would refuse to heed their cry, if they
did repent; but He knew they would not. They were given over to
hardness of heart and to a seared conscience.

A little parable follows in verses 7 and 8 before the reassuring
words of the close of the passage at which we have already looked.
Two plots of ground are seen side by side. The soil is alike in each
field; the same sun shines upon them both; they are refreshed by the
same showers. But at harvest time, one produces a fine crop that is a
delight to the farmer's heart; the other bears only thorns and briars
fit for the fire. What makes the difference?

In the one, the good seed had found acceptance, but not in the
other. The application is easy. Two boys grow up side by side. They
attend the same synagogue; later both come under Christian influence; they go to the same meetings; they hear the same preaching;
they see the same signs and wonders wrought by the Spirit of God;
they both feel His convicting power; they alike profess to believe in
His Name; both are baptized; both sit at the Supper of the Lord. But
when fiery persecution breaks out against the infant church, one
basely deserts the cause, while the other stands firm as a rock. The
reason is easy to discern. One has received the good seed into an
honest heart. The other has only made a lip profession, based on a
mere intellectual and emotional acquaintance with Christian truth.

It is the same in Hebrews 10, verses 26-35: "For if we sin wilfully after that we have received the knowledge of the truth, there remaineth no more sacrifice for sins, but a certain fearful looking for
of judgment, and fiery indignation, which shall devour the adver-
saries. He that despised Moses' law died without mercy under two
or three witnesses: of how much sorer punishment, suppose ye,

103

shall he be thought worthy, who hath trodden under foot the Son of God, and hath counted the blood of the covenant, wherewith he was sanctified, an unholy thing, and hath done despite unto the Spirit of grace? For we know Him that hath said, Vengeance belongeth unto Me, I will recompense, said the Lord. And again, The Lord shall judge His people. It is a fearful thing to fall into the hands of the living God.

"But call to remembrance the former days, in which, after ye were illuminated, ye endured a great fight of afflictions; and partly, whilst ye were made a gazingstock, both by reproaches and afflictions; and partly, whilst ye became companions of them that were so used. For ye had compassion of me in my bonds, and took joyfully the spoiling of your goods, knowing in yourselves that ye have in heaven a better and an enduring substance. Cast not away therefore your confidence, which hath great recompense of reward."

Here too, in the closing part of the passage, those to whom the author of Hebrews writes are assured of the reality of their faith. He does not use such strong language to stumble any. Even the weakest babe in Christ is safe in Him. Divinely illumined, these Hebrews had suffered and endured, not only individually, but they had strengthened the hands of others. Their reward was sure if they pressed firmly onward, knowing that they had a home in heaven that was eternally secure. Read carefully again verses 32-36, and remember that salvation is by grace, and reward is for service.

Then note the warning of the previous verses. The wilful sin is, of course, apostasy. It is turning from Christ after having made definite acquaintance with His truth. Such people deliberately trod the Son of God beneath their feet and counted His precious blood—on the basis of which God could look upon them as set aside for blessing—as a common or unholy thing, of no more value than the blood of beasts of old. What can God do with, or for, those who thus spurn His grace? They refuse His lovingkindness. Therefore they must know His wrath.

These Hebrews might reason thus: 'Even if Christianity is from heaven, yet the same is true of Judaism. If we turn away from Jesus, we do not turn from God. If we reject Calvary, we can go back to the sacrifice at the Temple.' But no, "there remaineth no more [that is, no other] sacrifice for sins." God cannot receive now the sacrifices of bulls and of goats since His own Son has fulfilled all the types by offering Himself without spot, a ransom for all who trust in Him. To refuse Him and to turn from His one sacrifice for sins was to expose oneself to a fearful looking for of judgment and fiery indignation which must destroy His enemies.

Though the majority of the company who professed to know Jesus as Saviour and Messiah were real, there was always, as today, the possibility that some were not genuine. So in chapter 12 the warning is repeated, but from a somewhat different standpoint. Note verses 15-17: "Looking diligently lest any man fail of the grace of God; lest any root of bitterness springing up trouble you, and thereby many be defiled; lest there be any fornicator, or profane person, as Esau, who for one morsel of meat sold his birthright. For ye know how that afterward, when he would have inherited the blessing, he was rejected: for he found no place of repentance, though he sought it carefully with tears."

Esau is the outstanding example of one who had full knowledge of the covenant of grace, but who in the hour of stress put a higher value on personal comfort than on the blessing of the Lord. When awakened at last to see his folly in some measure, he wept and pleaded for the blessing he had once bargained away; but it was too late. His father had given the blessing to Jacob, and could not repent.

This, as I understand it, is what is meant by the solemn words, "he found no place of repentance, though he sought it carefully with tears." It is not that he himself could not repent of his former levity and profaneness; but he could not find a place of repentance in the mind of his father. However badly Jacob had acted, Isaac now knew it was the will of God that the blessing of Abraham should be given to the younger son. The lesson is a serious one. Divine things are not to be trifled with. Mercies despised at one time may be sought in vain later on. It behooves us all to be real, to be in earnest about spiritual matters while it is called today. In this vein, the poet has written:

> *"Time is earnest, passing by,*
> *Death is earnest, drawing nigh.*
> *Sinner, wilt thou trifling be?*
> *Time and death appeal to thee."*

13
Repentance and Forgiveness

We may be instructed as to the how and when of divine forgiveness if we consider carefully what the Scriptures teach as to our own attitude toward our sinning brethren. This will emphasize anew what has come before us so frequently in these studies. While God gives remission of sins on the principle of pure grace, based on the work our Lord Jesus has accomplished when on the cross He provided a righteous ground upon which God could be just and yet the justifier of sinners who trust His Son, nevertheless this forgiveness is not granted to unrepentant sinners. His heart is always toward all men, but He does not force His pardoning grace on anyone. The moment the trembling sinner comes to Him, confessing His guilt and judging himself as utterly lost and unworthy, thus taking the ground of repentance, God speaks peace through Jesus Christ.

> *"The sinner who believes is free,*
> *Can say the Saviour died for me,*
> *Can point to the atoning blood*
> *And say, This made my peace with God."*

He who is thus forgiven is then called on to forgive those who sin against him. The prayer, "Forgive us our debts, as we forgive our debtors," is not a prayer for the lips of a lost sinner. It is the cry of a disciple. Forgiven eternally, the believer nevertheless needs daily forgiveness when, as an erring child of God, he grieves the Holy Spirit by allowing any unholy thing in his life. And he is therefore exhorted to forgive as God in Christ has forgiven him. He who refuses to show grace to an erring brother cannot enter into the joy of his own forgiveness by God.

This was hard for Peter to comprehend, and doubtless also for the other apostles. As spokesman for them all, Peter asked, "Lord, how oft shall my brother sin against me, and I forgive him? until seven times?" Seven was to Peter the number of spiritual and mystical perfection, but how feebly did he enter into the perfection of the grace that should characterize the child of the new creation. The reply of Jesus is challenging in its comprehensiveness, for it shows not only what should be the extent of our forgiveness in dealing with our fellow sinners, but it surely suggests the illimitable mercy that God our Father exercises towards us. He answered, "I say not unto thee, Until seven times; but Until seventy times seven" (Mt. 18:21-22). This is from the account as we have it in Matthew's Gospel, and it is immediately after this that we have the parable of the implacable servant who, forgiven himself, refused to show mercy to his fellow servants and found himself delivered to the tormentors; for governmental forgiveness in the house of God may be revoked if the object of it behaves unworthily afterwards. In this respect it is altogether different from eternal forgiveness.

Matthew gives the scope of forgiveness, but does not tell us anything concerning the attitude of the sinning brother who is to be the recipient of such grace. When we turn to Luke 17:3-4, we learn the terms upon which this forgiveness is to be granted. "Take heed to yourselves: If thy brother trespass against thee, rebuke him; and if he repent, forgive him. And if he trespass against thee seven times in a day, and seven times in a day turn again to thee, saying, I repent; thou shalt forgive him." Christian forgiveness is not to be confounded with indifference to evil. The brother who trespasses is to be rebuked, and that for his own good. In the Law, it was written, "Thou shalt in any wise rebuke thy neighbor, and not suffer sin upon him" (Lev. 19:17). It might be far easier simply to ignore the wrong done and pay no attention to the evildoer. But this is not God's way. He would have His children be imitators of Himself. He brings their sins home to them, thus seeking to arouse the conscience and create a sense of need; for, until they are conscious of sin, there will be no desire for forgiveness, nor true self-judgment.

When the guilty one has faced his sin, Jesus adds, "If he repent, forgive him." Again, let me stress what so often has come before us in this discussion. There is nothing meritorious in repentance; it is simply the recognition of the true state of affairs. So long as this is ignored, the offender will not seek pardon. When he honestly faces conditions as they are and comes confessing his sin, he is to be forgiven.

But note the extent of all this; the many times that such grace may have to be manifested is almost staggering. We read in verse 4, "And if he trespass against thee seven times in a day, and seven times in a day turn again to thee saying, I repent; thou shalt forgive him." If we, with all our personal sinfulness and shortcomings, are to forgive to this extent, how illimitable is the grace that our God waits to lavish on those who come to Him, saying, "I repent." There are no bounds to His restoring mercy.

Are we not all inclined to limit Him in this? Have we not said in our hearts, if not with our lips, 'I have failed so often. I have sinned so frequently. I am ashamed to come to Him again for forgiveness when I have proven myself so unworthy of His loving favor in the past.' But, if you were to prove yourself worthy, then His forgiveness would not be grace. He forgives because of the worthiness of Christ. He only waits for His sinning child to say, "I repent."

But if we thus need to go to Him so frequently when conscious that we have dishonored His holy Name, how gracious should be our attitude toward others. I am persuaded there are many of God's dear children who know very little of real fellowship with the Father simply because they cherish the memory of wrongs, real or imagined, which they will not forgive. 'Oh,' exclaims one, 'if you knew how terribly he has injured me, you would not wonder that I cannot forgive him. If he had not spoken so ill of me or acted so badly, it would be easy to forgive; but the offense is too great.' What strange nonsense is this for a child of grace to utter! Why, if you had not been wronged, there would be no occasion to forgive. It is because you have been trespassed against that you are called on to show the grace of God to the offender.

109

But perhaps we should be thinking more of the other side in this matter. Am I the one who has done the wrong? And am I refusing to repent? Then I have no right to expect forgiveness, and my Father Himself will not grant it until I can say from the heart, "I repent." No, my very gifts are so defiled that God cannot accept my attempts at worship and praise until I repent. The Saviour has said, "If thou bring thy gift to the altar, and there rememberest that thy brother hath ought against thee, leave there thy gift before the altar, and go thy way; first be reconciled to thy brother, and then come and offer thy gift" (Mt. 5:23-24). This is an abiding principle that transcends all dispensations. Yet how frequently is it ignored.

In many of the assemblies of God's saints, there are brothers, and sisters too, who have been estranged from each other for years. Forgetting that sin never dies of old age, they have sought to ignore wrongs done years ago, and to justify themselves in an un-Christ-like attitude to each other. With sins and trespasses unconfessed toward each other and toward God, they offer strange fire on His altar and fancy He receives the money they give ostensibly for His work and the worship they offer in His house.

But He will have none of it. To Him it is all an abomination. He is of purer eyes than to behold iniquity. He will be sanctified in them that come near Him. He says, "Go ye, and learn what that meaneth, I will have mercy, and not sacrifice." When wrongs are put right, when sins are confessed, when tears of repentance take the place of formal lip service, He will accept the offerings that are brought to His altar and give "beauty for ashes and the oil of joy for mourning and the garment of praise for the spirit of heaviness."

We speak of the need of revival, we sing of revival, we pray for revival; but the heavens seem as brass above our heads. We could have revival and blessing tomorrow if we were willing to pay the price. "Be zealous therefore, and repent."

Another practical illustration, a fully authentic narrative related to me by eye and ear witnesses who participated in the revival described, will perhaps enforce this more clearly than a further attempt at didactic instruction. In a community that shall be nameless, there had been a long period of spiritual famine and dearth. Years before a church had been born there in a time of great awakening, when the Spirit of God had worked powerfully and hundreds had been brought to repentance and had found peace with God. Bound together in the love of the Spirit, they had been a witnessing assembly whose testimony had borne abundant fruit through the whole district. Missionaries had gone out from their midst with hearts of flame and tongues of fire to carry the gospel to adjacent regions and even to faraway lands.

But all this was in the distant past. A period of coldness and powerlessness had followed that of the warmth of early days, and though the same people came together for the regularly announced meetings, all was formal and lifeless, except that a little group who mourned over the fallen estate of the church met from time to time to weep before God and to entreat Him to refresh His thirsty heritage. It was doubtless in answer to their prayers that two devoted men of God came among them for what were euphemistically called "revival services," though it was soon manifest that the true spirit of revival was conspicuously absent. Nevertheless, for a period of three weeks the crowds thronged the largest obtainable building, where the singing was hearty and the preaching clear and convincing. Yet there were no apparent conversions, although the evangelists pleaded with men to be reconciled to God and faithfully endeavored to win the lost to Christ.

At last, oppressed in spirit by conditions that seemed inexplicable, it was announced that for a time there would be no more preaching, but, instead, a day of fasting and prayer, to be followed by others if necessary until God Himself would reveal the hindrances and remove them.

To describe the exercises of that day of waiting on God would be impossible. There was much in the way of individual confession and crying to Him to make bare His arm in the restoration of backslidden saints and the awakening of the Christless. At the night meeting, the building was crowded, but there was no address. One after another prayed, some in agony of spirit, that God might come in. Suddenly a period of solemn silence was broken by a loud sobbing, and a strong man, an elder in the church, rose to his feet. "Brethren," he cried, "I am the one who has been hindering the blessing. I am the stumbling block in this community." Then he openly confessed that for years he had cherished malice and hatred in his heart against a fellow elder who had been at one time his bosom friend. There had been a dispute over a property line in which he claimed he had been cheated out of a few feet of land. Wrangling had led to increased bitterness. Strife had gone on for months, and when at last the matter was settled in the courts, it left him with a heart filled with hatred against his brother.

Striding across the front of the building, he offered his hand to this man who had also risen to his feet and, amid tears, declared it was he who was to blame rather than the other. Together they both went to the foot of the speaker's platform and dropped to their knees, confessing their sins and forgiving each other.

The effect on the vast crowd was marvelous. It was the beginning of a mighty work of grace in that town, the good results of which were recognized for years afterwards. Many who had been under deep conviction, but who had been stumbled by the unworthy conduct of these two leaders, soon joined them at the front, and the vast hall resounded with the cries of penitents and the glad songs of those who were led to rejoice in God's salvation. To the two who for so long had stood in the way of others and whose lives had been so barren and fruitless came new experiences of restoration and usefulness as their old-time spiritual fervor returned. This is no imaginary tale, and I am persuaded that in many a place there would be similar, or even greater, blessing if there were downright honesty in dealing with God and with one another.

Often have I heard the question discussed, Is there any possibility of another great worldwide revival before the Lord's return? Some have insisted that we are too near the end of the age to expect anything of the kind. Others are more optimistic as they point out that it would be in keeping with God's mercy to give one last powerful witness to His grace before the coming of our Lord Jesus

Christ and our gathering together unto Him. But after all, we do not need to discuss the pros and cons relating to worldwide revival. We should rather be concerned about revival in our own individual lives, and in our local assemblies. And surely it is never too late to seek for this. God is waiting to hear the cry of repentant hearts and to give showers of blessing where there is recognized need and a readiness to obey His Word.

The hindrances are all on our side, never on His. The great trouble is, we are so unreal, so self-satisfied, so little exercised as to our true condition in His sight. Shall we not come to Him as repentant supplicants, crying with the psalmist, "Wilt Thou not revive us again, that Thy people may rejoice in Thee?" Then with every doubtful thing cast aside, with every known sin confessed and judged, we shall prove the truth of the words, "The joy of the Lord is your strength." And as we thus joy in Him and He in us, we shall commend His lovingkindness to others and have the added gladness of leading needy sinners to His feet.

"Let us search and try our ways, and turn again to the Lord." He is waiting to be gracious. We are robbing Him of what is rightfully His if we hold anything back. He has said, "Bring ye all the tithes into the storehouse, that there may be meat in Mine house, and prove Me now herewith, saith the Lord of hosts, if I will not open you the windows of heaven, and pour you out a blessing, that there shall not be room enough to receive it. And I will rebuke the devourer for your sakes, and he shall not destroy the fruits of your ground; neither shall your vine cast her fruit before the time in the field, saith the Lord of hosts. And all nations shall call you blessed: for ye shall be a delightsome land, saith the Lord of hosts" (Mal. 3:10-12).

What will be fulfilled literally for Israel, when they at last meet His conditions, we may enter into spiritually in the present if we give Him His rightful place and deal resolutely with every evil thing in our hearts and lives as His searching light reveals it to us.

14
Hopeless Repentance

The tragedy of Judas is unquestionably the saddest story of human sin and perfidy ever recorded. That one could be in the chosen circle of the intimate friends and disciples of Jesus for over three years, listening to His teaching, beholding the works of power that He wrought, and observing the divinely perfect holiness of His life, and then become His betrayer, seems almost unbelievable. And yet there the record stands in God's Holy Word, and it will stand forever: "Judas by transgression fell, that he might go to his own place" (Acts 1:25).

We know nothing of his early years except that he was a man of Kerioth, for this is really the meaning of Iscariot. Kerioth was a city of Judea, so we learn from this that he was not, like the rest of the Twelve, a Galilean. He was a Judean, and in all probability had a measure of culture and refinement beyond that of the group of northern fishermen and villagers who, with him, made up the apostolic band. Like the others, his first public act of obedience to the call of God was in response to the Baptist's preaching of repentance. When the publicans and sinners justified God, being baptized with the baptism of John, Judas took his place among them. He too stepped down into the mystical river of judgment and submitted to the rite which was intended to show that he acknowledged himself a repentant sinner and was now looking for redemption in Israel.

What his inmost thoughts really were at this solemn crisis in his life we cannot tell, but we know he began as a disciple of John, for when Peter called for nominations for the vacated office of Judas, he reminded his fellow disciples that, "of these men which have companied with us all the time that the Lord Jesus went in and out among us, beginning from the baptism of John, unto that same day that He was taken up from us, must one be ordained to be a witness with us of His resurrection" (Acts 1:21-22). The necessary inference is that Judas himself had answered to this and that they had known him from the baptism of John until his terrible defection. We do not have any particulars of his call to be one of the Twelve, but there are several others of the company of whom this is also true. In fact, only in the cases of Andrew and Peter, John and James, Philip and Nathaniel, and Matthew the publican, are we given direct information as to how they came to be numbered with the selected group.

It is noticeable that in the lists of the Twelve as given by each of the Synoptics (Mt. 10:2-4; Mk. 3:14-19; Lk. 6:13-16) his name comes last, and in each instance attention is directed to him by the words, "who also betrayed him," or, as Luke puts it, "which also was the traitor." What a terrible designation to stand for eternity!

As to the esteem in which he was held by the rest, before his wickedness became known, it is only necessary to say that he was the treasurer of this little group of itinerant preachers, dependent on the bounty of those who responded to their message for daily bread. He "had the bag" and John tells us he "bare what was put therein." The words imply that he misappropriated a part of the common fund. And yet he was trusted. Even Jesus, who needed not that any should testify of men for He knew what was in man, patiently bore with him through the years of his ill-doing when, Gehazi-like, he thought he was covering up his tracks.

Not only was he the apostolic bursar, but he had the honorable position of almoner. It was he who was appointed to minister to the poor. On the occasion when Jesus ate the last Passover with His disciples and turned to Judas, saying, "That thou doest, do quickly," none suspected what he really referred to. As the traitor passed out into the night, they thought he had gone at the Lord's behest to give something to the needy.

To what extent he was sincere when he went forth as one of the Twelve, to preach that men should repent and to prepare them for the manifestation of the King, we cannot say and speculation would be useless. But he was with the rest when they exultingly declared, "Lord, even the demons are subject unto us." Did he question or shudder when the Master bade them not rejoice because of this, wonderful as it was, but rather that their names were written in heaven?

Thomas DeQuincey, Marie Corelli, and other *literati* have sought to build up a defense for Judas and have even attempted to make a well-intentioned but disappointed hero of him. They even go so far as to intimate that the betrayal was, after all, not a positive act of treachery, but simply the ill-considered but well-meant effort of a live man of affairs to commit Jesus to a course for which He was destined, as Iscariot honestly believed, but which His humility and indecision made Him slow to take. Such reasoning is preposterous and borders on blasphemy, for it impugns the wisdom and obedience of Jesus Himself, who was ever the Father's delight, doing always those things that pleased Him.

Judas never had a true love for Christ. The incident of the alabaster box of spikenard makes that perfectly evident. To Mary there was nothing too good for Jesus. So she took her woman's treasure, the box of precious ointment, broke it and poured it upon His head, as He said in deep appreciation of her devotion, for His burial, of which she had probably learned while sitting at His feet. But to Judas, and to others who were more or less influenced by him, this was utter waste. With cool calculation he figured that the ointment if sold would have yielded three hundred *denarii*, a full year's wages for a Roman soldier or an ordinary laboring man. Cunningly he insinuated that it was wasted on Jesus when it might have relieved much human misery if given to the poor. But it was only to cover up the covetousness of his heart that he mentioned the poor. He was really calculating the use he could have made of so large a sum for his own ends.

Such a man proved to be a ready tool in the hands of a designing and corrupt priesthood. His itching palms would make it easy for him to agree to sell the Lord into their hands for thirty pieces of silver. Did he recall the prophecy of Zechariah as to that, or was he so

117

blinded and had he become so insensate through covetousness that the prophet's words had gone from his memory, if he ever knew them? He probably fulfilled them unconsciously, as he also fulfilled certain prophetic passages in the Psalms, notably, "He that eateth bread with Me hath lifted up his heel against Me."

Note his perfect self-command and lack of telltale change of color when all were gathered around the table and Jesus informed them that one of their number should betray Him. Judas asked coolly, "Is it I?" and gave no sign of an accusing conscience. Even the reference to the sop and the grace that led the Lord to give him the choice portion left him unmoved as before. He arose from that feast of love and went out—and it was night. Not only was it night in the natural sense, but it was dark, dark night in his soul, to be unrelieved forevermore. He had turned his back forever on the light. Satan had definitely entered into him. He was under control of the spirit that energetically works in the children of disobedience. Christ's words are full of meaning, "Have not I chosen you twelve, and one of you is a devil?"

It would seem that just as one may yield himself to God and thus be filled and dominated by the Holy Spirit, so one can hand himself over to the authority of darkness and be controlled by Satan himself. It was thus with Judas. Any qualms of conscience he had ever known were ended now. Any kindly regard for Jesus which had ever held sway in his breast was now forever stifled. Any tenderness of heart he had ever experienced was now changed to hardness like that of the nether millstone. He was sold under sin in the fullest sense. For him there could now be no turning back until his nefarious plot was executed in all its horrid details. The receiving of the money from the wily priests, the guiding of the mob to Gethsemane's shades, the effrontery that led him to walk boldly forward, exclaiming, "Hail, Master!" as he planted a hypocritical kiss on His cheek—all these tell of a conscience seared and a heart that had become adamant in wickedness.

But even for Judas there came an awakening at last. When he saw how meekly the Saviour allowed them to maltreat and condemn

118

Him, his sensibilities were stirred, and although there was no turning to God, he regretted his fearful error. I cannot do better than let Matthew himself tell the story:

"Then Judas, which had betrayed Him, when he saw that He was condemned, repented himself, and brought again the thirty pieces of silver to the chief priests and elders, saying, I have sinned, in that I have betrayed the innocent blood. And they said, What is that to us? see thou to that. And he cast down the pieces of silver in the temple, and departed, and went and hanged himself. And the chief priests took the silver pieces, and said, It is not lawful for to put them into the treasury, because it is the price of blood. And they took counsel, and bought with them the potter's field, to bury strangers in. Wherefore that field was called, The field of blood, unto this day."

Since Judas repented, was he not forgiven and will he not after all find a place with the blest, even though in his despair he filled a suicide's grave? Our Lord's own words forbid any such conclusion. He declared, when speaking of Judas, "Good were it for that man if he had never been born." This negates any possibility of salvation for him in another world; for, in spite of the enormity of his guilt, if he ever attained to the joys of paradise, it would have been well for him to be born.

The fact is, the Holy Spirit, who selects His words with divine meticulousness, used an altogether different word here, from that which we have been considering, for repentance. It is not *metanoia* but *metamellomai*— not a change of mind which involves a new attitude toward sin and self and God, but "to care afterwards," that is, to be regretful or remorseful. Thousands of imprisoned convicts, guilty of most atrocious crimes, repent in this lower sense. They would give much if they had not committed the offenses for which they are now suffering the penalty of the law, but they have never bowed the knee to God nor confessed their guilt to Him. So with Judas. He acknowledged his folly and wickedness to the callous priests who contemptuously replied, "What is that to us? see thou to that," and then were very punctilious as to the use they should make of the "tainted money" thrown down at their feet. But Judas went into eternity without one word with God regarding his sin or one evidence of repentance unto life.

Remorse is not repentance toward God. It brings no pardon, no remission of sins. It is but the terrible aftermath of a course of persistent rejection of the Word of the Lord, which, while it leaves the soul in an agony of bitter sorrow over opportunities forever lost and grace despised, works no change in the conscience but leaves it unpurged forever. It is in this connection that the history of Judas becomes so important for us. It is God's own warning signal to all who tamper with His truth and grace. To play fast and loose with divine revelation is fatal. Its dire effects abide forever.

There is a soft, easy-going philosophy, much in vogue in our day, that would give men hope of a purifying repentance after death, no matter what state they might be in when life's day is ended. But the case of Judas is the negative answer to all this. Nothing he had ever heard from the lips of the Son of God during those years of intimate association with Him gave the remorseful traitor one ray of hope when he at the last began to apprehend something of the fearful wrong he had done. In his harrowing despair, he turned not to God, but sought to get farther away from Him, and rushed out of the world a self-murderer.

Some have fancied they detected a discrepancy between Matthew's account of his death and that given by Peter in the Upper Room. But the two passages are easily pieced together. Judas hanged himself, probably in the very plot of ground purchased by the priests for the thirty pieces of silver. Suspended from a tree, the bough to which the rope was tied in all likelihood broke and he fell to the ground, rupturing his abdomen as he did so, so that "all his bowels gushed out." It is easy to visualize the horrid scene.

What an end to the life of one who had been numbered with the Twelve, but what an unspeakably awful introduction to an unending eternity of woe! Judas is somewhere today. He will exist throughout the ages. And never will he be able to lose sight of the face of the One whom he betrayed and of the cross upon which He died. But memory will not cleanse his soul. Though the victim of a remorse that must become increasingly poignant as the eons roll on, his must ever be a hopeless repentance because it is based, not on a sense of the wrong done to God, but of the wretchedness in which he involved himself by his stupendous folly.

Byron has written:

> *"There are wanderers o'er the sea of eternity,*
> *Whose bark drives on and on,*
> *And anchored ne'er shall be."*

Judas, not Iscariot, has described such as "wandering stars, to whom is reserved the blackness of darkness forever" (Jude 13). Those who refuse to turn to God in repentance while grace is freely offered are destined to repent when all hope has fled and they shall be as stars eternally out of their orbit. Created to circle round the Sun of Righteousness, they have gone off on a tangent of self-will, and despite all the constraining power of the love of Christ, shall plunge deeper and deeper into the outer darkness, driving ever on, farther and farther from the One whom they have spurned and whose mercy they have rejected. It is an alarming picture, and God meant it to be such, for He would not have any man trifle with sin. He desires that all should turn to Him and live.

It brings us face to face with what we saw before, that character tends to permanence. Men so accustom themselves to certain courses that they lose all desire to change, even though they may realize their behavior entails misery and woe. Hell itself is but the condition that men choose for themselves at last made permanent. By their own volition they unfit themselves for the society of the good and the blessed. Moreover, they reject the opportunity for the impartation of a new life and nature by a second birth which would make them suited to God in order that they would be at home in His society. So there is nothing before them but "everlasting destruction from the presence of the Lord, and from the glory of His power; when He shall come to be glorified in His saints, and to be admired in all them that believe (because our testimony among you was believed) in that day" (2 Thess. 1:9-10).

It is true that God is love, and that He wills not the death of the sinner, but that all should turn to Him and live. It is equally true that He is light; and sin unjudged and unconfessed cannot abide the blaze of His glory, but must seek its own dark level. Of the lost it is written, "These shall go away into everlasting punishment." It implies, in a sense, a certain voluntariness on their part. Unfitted to abide in the light, like bats and other creatures of the night, they seek, like the infidel Altamont, a hiding place from God. It was he who is reported to have cried when dying, "O, Thou blasphemed and yet indulgent God! Hell itself were a refuge if it hide me from Thy face." Men can sin till, as Whittier so aptly puts it, they "lack the will to turn." For them there may be endless remorse, but no true repentance toward God, and therefore no hope forevermore.

15
City-Wide Repentance

While repentance is distinctly an individual exercise, yet we have in the Word of God, as we have already seen, churches called on to repent, and we learn from our Lord's words, in Matthew 12:41 and Luke 11:32, of the repentance of a city: "The men of Nineveh shall rise in judgment with this generation, and shall condemn it; because they repented at the preaching of Jonas; and, behold, a greater than Jonas is here."

This is most suggestive, particularly in view of the failure of the cities wherein Christ had done most of His wondrous miracles, to turn to God. "If," He declared, "the mighty works which have been done in you had been done in Tyre and Sidon, they would have repented in sackcloth and ashes." This was one of the passages that caused great distress of mind and absolute bewilderment to the sensitive souls of Charlotte Bronte and her gifted sisters. If Tyre and Sidon would have repented under such circumstances, why did not a loving God give them a similar testimony in order that they might have been saved from destruction? One answer of course is, that the men and women of these ancient cities will be judged at last only for rejecting the light they had, and not on the ground of knowledge they did not possess.

But from these Scriptures we learn that a city in God's sight is a responsible entity, and that He holds it accountable to obey His word and walk in His truth. This raises a question as to how far ministers of Christ ought to concern themselves about the sins of the cities wherein they labor, and to what extent they should lift up their voices against the evils of the day, when tolerated by those in authority. Many preachers take the ground that the servant of God is to confine himself wholly to explaining the gospel and to calling individual sinners to repentance. The Lord will deal with civic unrighteousness in His own way and time, we are told, and it is best that pastors and evangelists ignore what it is not in their province or power to correct.

And yet God has unquestionably set His seal in a remarkable manner on the efforts of some of His honored servants who in their day and generation battled against entrenched wickedness in civic and national affairs. Think of the influence exerted for righteousness by Savonarola in Florence, Calvin in Geneva, Luther in Erfurt, Knox in Edinburgh, Wesley in London and all England, and a host of like-minded men who cried out unflinchingly against the iniquities of the times in which they lived. It is written, "The wicked flee when no man pursueth." But our own Dr. Charles H. Parkhurst, whose name was a terror to privileged sin, well exclaimed, "But they go a lot faster when the righteous get after them."

The prophets of old were set by God over cities and peoples and nations to call them to account for their evil-doing and to summon them to prepare to meet their God. The Saviour, as we have noted, dealt with cities as such, and nothing is more pathetic than His lament over unrepentant Jerusalem: "And when He was come near, He beheld the city, and wept over it, saying, If thou hadst known, even thou, at least in this thy day, the things which belong unto thy peace! but now they are hid from thine eyes. For the days shall come upon thee, that thine enemies shall cast a trench about thee, and compass thee round, and keep thee in on every side, and shall lay thee even with the ground, and thy children within thee; and they shall not leave in thee one stone upon another; because thou knewest not the time of thy visitation" (Lk. 19:41-44). Link with this His impassioned cry as recorded in Matthew 23:37-39: "O Jerusalem, Jerusalem, thou that killest the prophets, and stonest them which are sent unto thee, how often would I have gathered thy children together, even as a hen gathereth her chickens under her wings, and ye would not! Behold, your house is left unto you desolate. For I say unto you, Ye shall not see Me henceforth, till ye shall say, Blessed is He that cometh in the name of the Lord." Surely none can read such passages as these without recognizing the civic consciousness of Jesus. He yearned over men, not only as individuals needing personal salvation, but as community groups which would be blest on earth if they would only heed God's Word and repent.

To many of us the story of the repentance of Nineveh is far more wonderful than that of the miracle of Jonah and the sea monster. People object to the latter as being unheard of elsewhere and so contrary to ordinary human knowledge that it is unbelievable. But where else in all human history do we find a great, godless, pleasure-loving city brought to its knees as in the case of Nineveh? If it were not written in the Word of God and so definitely authenticated by our Lord Himself (as also the instance of the experience of Jonah) we might hesitate to credit it. But here it is, solemnly recorded on the pages of Holy Writ.

A great city containing "six score thousand souls that knew not their right hand from their left"—that is, little children—must have had a very large adult population indeed. This vast throng were given over to impiety and wickedness of such gross nature that God could tolerate it no longer and sent His prophet to announce its summary destruction. As in the case of the cities of the plain, whose stench had reached to heaven, He would blot Nineveh from the face of the earth. But the Word of the Lord came home so convincingly to the hearts of the king and his councillors of state that they not only repented themselves, but called on all in the city to do the same. The results were unparalleled in the history of religious revivals. The entire populace fell down before the Lord in sackcloth and ashes, bemoaning their sins and crying for mercy. And God heard and pardoned—much to the disgust of Jonah, who was more concerned about his own prophetic reputation than about the salvation of an entire people.

Perhaps the nearest thing to this in secular history is the story of Savonarola and Florence, Italy. The impassioned monk, moved to deepest concern by the lasciviousness, the licentiousness, and the godless luxury of the Florentines, inveighed against the city, threatening dire judgment from heaven if there were no repentance, and moved the populace almost as one man. Drawing his messages largely from the last solemn book of the Bible, he preached expository addresses on the Apocalypse in the Duomo month after month. The awful figures of judgment depicted therein he declared to be about to find their fulfillment on the Florentines and all Italy unless the people repented and turned from their corrupt behavior.

Nobles, merchants, and laborers alike felt the power of his words and at his call they brought their treasures of gold, jewels, and objects of art and piled them in the public square at his feet, to be sold or distributed for the relief of the poor and needy. The churches were crowded with penitent suppliants confessing their sins and seeking divine forgiveness. For a time at least, the city was largely purged from its iniquity and men realized their responsibility to seek to glorify God in their lives and with their means, instead of living in lusts and pleasures on the earth.

It is true Savonarola was burned at the stake in the end, because of the hatred of a corrupt clergy; in that he but shared the baptism of his Lord and participated in His cup of sorrow. He was, undoubtedly, the most Christlike man of his generation, and he suffered as his Master suffered because he was a witness to the truth. His own words were really prophetic: "A Christian's life consists in doing good and suffering evil." After the lapse of centuries, the church that decreed his martyrdom honored him as one of its outstanding apostles. Like Israel of old, the fathers slew him and the children built his sepulcher. So it ever is in this inconstant world.

Calvin's outward regeneration of Geneva is another marked instance of the power of the Word—when faithfully proclaimed—to influence civic life. Unhappily there was a great deal of Old Testament legality about it all, and like most men who really amount to anything, Calvin made some stupendous blunders, as in the case of Servetus, for which the world has never forgiven him. But his influence throughout was on the side of righteousness and truth, and for this he will be remembered forever and shine as the stars eternally.

Macaulay declared that the Wesleyan revival saved England from the horrors of anarchy and revolution. Yet Wesley's great work was preaching the gospel and calling sinners to repentance. That message stirred London and the other great cities of Britain to their depths, and even where it did not result in actual conversion to God, it made people ashamed of the enormities they had condoned in church and state and led to a national renovation that was an untold blessing to millions.

Jonathan Edwards' clarion call to repentance and faith in God meant more to the young American nation than can now be computed. He put the fear of the Lord in men's hearts and this largely molded the character of the fathers of the republic.

After the terrible war between the states, the voice of D. L. Moody was heard throughout the land, and across the seas, arousing, heartening, and bringing spiritual deliverance to many thousands who had lost all that life held dear. Accounted Chicago's most prominent and most valued citizen for a generation, his influence for good in that great city was simply marvellous and, though more than another generation has passed since his voice was hushed in death, "he being dead yet speaketh" and his influence is perhaps greater today than when he was alive. His favorite text was, "He that doeth the will of God abideth forever," and since his death the truth of this has been increasingly manifest.

Observe carefully that these men, and many others whose names might be added to the illustrious list, wrought their works of power, not by mixing in political squabbles, but by faithfully preaching the Word of God, denouncing sin fearlessly and persistently, enjoining men to repent or face high Heaven in judgment, exalting Christ Jesus as the only Saviour and the supreme example for all who professed to follow Him, and insisting that outward forms and ceremonies could never satisfy an offended God. There must be true self-judgment, a turning to God from idols to serve Him wholly and to wait for His Son from heaven.

Such preaching inevitably produces results in reformation of life and purification of civic relationship. When the conscience is

127

reached and the will is so captivated by grace that men turn to the Lord and cleave to Him with purpose of heart, all other desirable results will soon manifest themselves.

What is needed in every city of every land is, not a mere "new deal" or a political reformation, but preachers of righteousness who will proclaim the Word of God, crying, "Thus saith the Lord," without fear or favor, faithfully dealing with the problems of the day in the light of the cross of Christ.

So long as ministers are afraid to expose the vices of the rich lest their collections shrink, or fear to cry aloud and spare not regarding such entrenched evils as the ruthless exploitation of labor, the horrors of prostitution, and the abominations of the liquor traffic, lest they offend some who perhaps directly or indirectly derive a part of their income from these very sources, the world will only despise them and think of them as what they really are, conscienceless sycophants toadying to the wealthy while they attempt superciliously to patronize the poor for outward effect.

On the other hand, the clerical demagogue, blatantly advocating godless schemes for the renovation of society that involve, if successful, the very destruction of the church of God itself, is beneath contempt. These men, as a rule, are unsaved and do not even pretend to be born again. Their place, if anywhere, is on the lecture platform, not in the pulpit which they degrade by their utterances. It is one of the amazing signs of our times that in many churches communistic propaganda and similar unscriptural plans for overturning the present unsatisfactory order of society are not only tolerated but applauded. Yet this philosophy is the avowed enemy of God and His Christ, and churches that nurture these enemies of the cross are sheltering in their bosoms vipers that, if not sternly dealt with, will sting them to death in the end.

Real Christianity is the truest friend the laboring man will ever know. It provides for happiness, not only in this life, but in the life that is to come. It respects sacredly the natural rights of all men, exhorting the rich to use their wealth for the blessing of their fellows and guiding the poor into paths of contentment and peace. The

128

gospel received makes the only real brotherhood that the world has ever seen. Tolstoi, disappointed to find how powerless his plausible theories were to move the hearts of men, exclaimed sadly, "I found out that there could never be a brotherhood without brothers." This is the great secret many of our Christless social reformers have never yet learned. Did ministers everywhere realize it, they would cease trying to work from the outside in, and would begin at once to work from the inside out. There will never be a regenerated society without regenerated individuals. Hence our Lord's stress on the heavenly birth: "Except a man be born again he cannot see [nor enter] the kingdom of God."

This Kingdom is not, as many religious leaders would have us believe, simply an idealistic state of human society. It is the aggregate of those who have humbled themselves before God as repentant sinners and received the Lord Jesus Christ as their own personal Saviour: "Being born again, not of corruptible seed, but of incorruptible, by the Word of God, which liveth and abideth forever. For all flesh is as grass, and all the glory of man as the flower of grass. The grass withereth, and the flower thereof falleth away: but the Word of the Lord endureth forever. And this is the Word which by the gospel is preached unto you" (1 Pet. 1:23-25).

Let all God-anointed preachers proclaim anew what Spurgeon called "the three R's"—Ruin, Regeneration, and Redemption, and we may hope to see again, not only individuals, but whole communities brought to repentance.

To this end, we need to get back to our Bibles and back to our knees. Let prayer meetings be re-established in churches where for years there has not been spiritual fervor sufficient to maintain them, and all kinds of entertainments have been substituted in their place. Let the Word of God be given its rightful place, and let ministers and people cease criticizing and sitting in judgment upon it; but, instead, let them study it carefully in dependence on the Holy Spirit for divine illumination. In the light of that Word, let our manner of life be sternly judged, putting away every known evil and confessing our past sin and failure. Then may we expect God to be gracious, to grant repentance unto life to cities long given over to our modern paganism, and so to bring again times of refreshing from the presence of the Lord.

The days are dark. The need is urgent. Men are dying all about us in their sins. The gospel is still the power of God unto salvation. Let it be faithfully preached, and it will do its work as of old. Nothing else has the same attractive power or will appeal so winsomely to the weary hearts and troubled souls of the men, women, and children, who make up our great, godless cities, whose appalling need should be a challenge to every preacher of the Word.

16
Preaching that Produces Repentance

In all that I have written, I have failed completely to express what was surging up in my soul if I have given anyone the impression that I think of repentance as something meritorious which must be produced in man by self-effort before he is fit to come to God for salvation. On the other hand, I hope I have made myself clear that it is the work of the Holy Spirit producing repentance, that leads any soul to come to Christ in order to be saved. The formula used by Paul the Apostle to describe the substance of his preaching ought to make this plain. He proclaimed to Jew and Gentile alike the necessity of "repentance toward God, and faith toward our Lord Jesus Christ."

Since this is the divine order, it behooves those of us who seek to give the gospel to a lost world to inquire as to the type of preaching that is best calculated to produce such results. In other words, what kind of message is needed to bring our hearers to repentance?

And in trying to answer this very proper inquiry, let me first say that it is not necessary invariably to use the actual term "repentance" in order to bring about this very much to be desired effect. In many quarters, men have attached to the words "repent" and "repentance" meanings that do not properly belong to them. So that there is the possibility that our hearers may altogether misunderstand us if we urge them, in so many words, to repent. They may imagine they must by some effort of their own, produce that which entitles them to consider that they have attained a state where they are acceptable to God. This is not the truth as set forth in His Word, as every Bible-taught preacher well knows.

But, on the other hand, it is not wise to be too squeamish about the use of an expression which we have seen to be eminently scriptural, and which the Holy Spirit Himself has used in all dispensations. John the Baptist and our Lord, the Twelve Apostles and Paul, preached that men should repent and do works meet for repentance; yet in no case did the thought of anything meritorious on man's part enter into it. Evidently the term used had not then been misapplied as it has been since. But what biblical expression is there that has not been perverted in the interest of some false system throughout the so-called Christian centuries? Such words as regeneration, justification, sanctification, yes, and even the very word salvation itself have all been grievously misused and the most unscriptural doctrines have been built upon them. Are we therefore to discard the terms themselves, or shall we not rather seek to present them in a right way, clarifying their meaning so far as we possibly can, in order that wrong conclusions may be averted?

So in the present case we want results. How best can men be brought to see their lost condition, and therefore to feel the need of the salvation God offers so freely in His blessed Son? In endeavoring so to preach as to bring this to pass, we are not shut up to one method of presentation, however, though the message must always be the same. God has only one remedy for man's lost condition and that is the gospel of His grace. But the manner in which this is set forth may differ according to the circumstances and the state of mind of the people addressed. Thus Paul was made all things to all men if by any means he might save some. And a somewhat careful analysis of the few sermons recorded in the book of the Acts will show us how differently the truth was proclaimed on different occasions.

Yet in one thing they all were alike in each instance Christ was lifted up; His life, His death, His resurrection, His glorious return personally, and His power to save, were plainly set forth. The one solitary exception seems, at first glance, to be Paul's sermon on Mars' Hill, in Athens. But we need to remember that he was interrupted by a mocking crowd before he had opportunity to finish. He began by a logical, calmly reasoned attempt to prove the unity of the Godhead and so to stress the sin of idolatry—for he was addressing a heathen people that they might realize their sin and folly. Then he announced that God, who in His patient grace had overlooked much of their past ignorance, "now commandeth all men everywhere to repent: because He hath appointed a day, in the which He will judge the world in righteousness, by that Man whom He hath ordained; whereof He hath given assurance unto all men, in that He hath raised Him from the dead" (Acts 17:30-31). He was now prepared to tell them more of the Lord Jesus and show how God had set Him forth as the one only Saviour. "And when they heard of the resurrection of the dead, some mocked: and others said, We will hear thee again of this matter" (v. 32). And so they turned contemptuously away, thus losing, perhaps forever, the opportunity of hearing the gospel of the grace of God, unfolded in all its beauty and power.

In Peter's sermons, on Pentecost and on the occasion of the healing of the lame man, he could bring directly home to his Jewish hearers their fearful guilt in rejecting the Redeemer whom God had sent, in accordance with the ancient oracles, to save and to bless by turning them away from their iniquities. In great power he pressed on them their responsibility in regard to Jesus, a responsibility they could not possibly evade.

In each instance, conviction gripped many who listened, they repented of the great sin of Christ-rejection, and identified themselves with Him whom now they confessed as Lord and Saviour by being baptized in His Name.

In Cornelius' house, the method of presentation was somewhat different, for Peter was there addressing a Gentile group. Nevertheless, they were a company who were, through Jewish contact, quite familiar with the hope of Israel. They had heard of Jesus, and of the treatment He had received at the hands of His own nation. Peter showed with all simplicity and clearness how every blessing was bound up with Him. He rehearsed the story of His wondrous life, His sacrificial death, and His triumph over the grave, climaxing all with the glorious message, "To Him give all the prophets witness, that through His name whosoever believeth in Him shall receive remission of sins" (Acts 10:43). During the time he was speaking, the hearts of his listeners had been responding to the truth. When he made this declaration, they, as one man, received the message and the Holy Spirit sealed and baptized them into the body of Christ.

It is true that repentance as such is not mentioned, but it is plainly implied. Turning from all else, these Gentiles trusted alone in Christ.

Paul, in the synagogue at Antioch in Pisidia, followed a similar outline, and with amazing results. It is a model sermon for all who would endeavor to preach the gospel today. There was no effort to be startling or original, no attempt at eloquence or rhetorical flourish, no pandering to the natural desire to win the approval of his audience. Solemnly, honestly, earnestly, he told the story of Jesus, and showed at the last that all hope for salvation was in Him and in Him alone: "Be it known unto you therefore, men and brethren, that through this Man is preached unto you the forgiveness of sins: and by Him, all that believe are justified from all things, from which ye could not be justified by the law of Moses" (Acts 13:38-39). Then, with a solemn warning of the judgment that must fall upon them if they spurned the message of grace, he brought his discourse to a close. The whole city seemed to be stirred by the sermon of the strange preacher, for the Gentiles begged that it might be repeated, at least in substance, to them on the next Sabbath, and the eventual result was that many were converted and a church established in that city before the Apostle and his companions moved on.

It is noteworthy that so simple a method of presentation should be accompanied with such power. But where the preacher is truly a godly man and seeks in the fear of God to show his hearers their need and then presents Christ—His person and His work—as the all-sufficient answer to their need, the Holy Spirit can be depended on to use the Word in producing conviction and leading to repentance.

The Epistle to the Romans, while not merely a sermon or homily, but rather a careful treatise, is the fullest unfolding of the Christian message given us in the Scriptures. It is true that in this letter we have the gospel taught rather than preached, and in a certain sense it is the evangel set forth for the understanding of the saints instead of for the salvation of sinners, yet God has used it, in whole or in part, to lead thousands to repent and believe in the Lord Jesus as their Saviour and Lord. He who would preach so as to produce these desirable results cannot do better than saturate his own soul and fill his own mind with the truth as it is set forth there.

How much Augustine in the fourth century and Luther in the sixteenth owed to this Epistle! It is the cornerstone of New Testament theology and the battleground of the Reformation. From the day that the Vicar-general, Staupitz, drew the monk Martin's attention to the key verse, "The just shall live by faith," it began to open up to the troubled spirit of the earnest young priest. Leading him to see the folly of trusting any righteousness of His own, and the blessedness of resting in the righteousness of God as revealed in the gospel, this was repentance indeed, never to be repented of!

In the opening chapters, the inspired writer brings all mankind, as it were, into the courtroom, and proves that all are sinners and guilty before God. The ignorant heathen are not to be judged for rejecting a Saviour of whom they have never heard, but they are already lost and guilty because of their own sins and will be judged accordingly. He deals with these sins unsparingly and in this becomes an example for all who would faithfully minister the truth to the souls of sinful men.

In the first part of the second chapter, he exposes the hypocrisy and wickedness of the more cultured, philosophic class who condemned and despised their more uncouth and barbaric fellows, while they themselves were slaves to enormities just as vile and abominable in the sight of God. Then he looks at the religious Jew, boasting in the Law and priding himself on being of the seed of Abraham, while his life is such that through him the Name of God is blasphemed among the Gentiles. He shows conclusively that none can ever hope to attain salvation on the ground of human merit or legal works, "For there is no difference between the Jew and the

Greek." "All have sinned, and come short of the glory of God." "There is none righteous, no, not one." The Law, which had been proposed as a test for life, had proven to be but a ministry of death and of condemnation. By disobedience all have come under judgment. No future reformation could atone for the past. All the world is brought in guilty before God.

Then comes the wonderful setting forth of the divine provision for man's desperate need. "But now"—having proven the unrighteousness of all men— "the righteousness of God [apart from] the law is manifested, being witnessed by the law and the prophets; even the righteousness of God, which is by faith of Jesus Christ, unto all and upon all them that believe."

Thus the question that perplexed Socrates was answered five hundred years later. Puzzled, he exclaimed, "It may be, Plato, that the Deity can forgive sins, but I do not see how." Christ's vicarious atonement is the righteous basis upon which God "can be just and the Justifier of him who believes on Jesus."

Why waste time on substitutes that can never move the conscience and produce repentance when the gospel is the dynamic of God unto salvation to everyone that believeth? This is the message for our unreal and hypercritical age, as truly as for every era of the past. Men talk of a new evangel for changing times. But the old story of Calvary still meets the needs of sinners—and Christ came not to call the righteous, but sinners, to repentance. Thousands can bear witness that they never realized how utterly lost and ruined they were until they saw themselves in the light of the cross of Jesus. No wonder Paul declared, "I determined not to know anything among you, save Jesus Christ, and Him crucified." The old hymn is right that says,

> *"I need no other argument,*
> *I want no other plea.*
> *It is enough that Jesus died,*
> *And that He died for me."*

Such was the gospel of Luther, that set half of Europe aflame with love for the Saviour and devotion to God. Such was the burning message of Whitefield, Edwards, and the Wesleys, that transformed untold thousands of lives in the days of the great awakening at the close of the Eighteenth Century.

Such was the story, which, told in living power by Jeremiah Meneely and his associates, shook Ireland and Scotland in the great revival of 1859-60.

Such was the trumpet call of Caughey and Finney and later of Dwight L. Moody, that brought tens of thousands to repentance in the mighty visitations of the Nineteenth Century in America and Britain.

Such was the forceful evangel of Reuben A. Torrey, J. Wilbur Chapman, and a host of other stalwarts as they visited Australia, New Zealand, Britain, and every corner of America in the early years of the present century.

Such was the flaming proclamation of that prince of preachers, Charles H. Spurgeon, as for a generation he ministered by tongue from his London pulpit, and by pen, to millions throughout the entire world.

And what shall I more say? The time would fail me to tell of Munhall, of A. C. Dixon, of Gypsy Smith, of Billy Sunday, of Mel Trotter, of the Stevens brothers, of Mordecai Ham, and scores of like-minded men of God, who in power have set forth man's sinfulness and God's great salvation through Christ's redemptive work, and thereby moved myriads to repentance.

The Salvation Army's marvelous success in its early days, in bringing the very vilest to find newness of life when they turned as confessed sinners to Christ, certainly did not rest on a carefully reasoned out theology preached in cultured phraseology, but in stressing the awfulness of sin and its dreadful penalty, and the wondrous grace that provides deliverance for all who will come to the Saviour and find cleansing in His blood.

How pitiable it is to see men, who ought to be winners of souls, turning away from this grand old gospel to the vapid puerilities of what is vaingloriously termed modern thought, and being content to preach on year after year without ever seeing a tear of repentance drop from the eyes of their hearers or moving any to cry in distress, "What must I do to be saved?"

Back to the gospel, brethren, if like the men of God throughout the centuries who have turned many to righteousness, you would bring men to repentance and lead them to heaven. This will never result from substituting a social service gospel, which is really no gospel at all, but an attempt to make the cross of Christ of none effect. By saying this I do not mean for one moment to cast a slur upon well-meant efforts to ameliorate conditions under which millions of our fellowmen are struggling. Everywhere that the pure evangel has found a home in human hearts it has bettered the social environment into which it has found its way. Even unsaved men profit by the love and grace set forth in the teaching of our Lord Jesus Christ. Men are ashamed to do in the light what they will do unblushingly in the dark, and so the gospel has curbed many social evils and bettered living conditions, wherever it has been received.

It was said of Paul and his companions when they entered a certain city, "These that have turned the world upside down are come hither also." The trouble with this fallen world is that it is wrong side up. It needs to be turned upside down in order to be right side up. And twenty centuries of missions and evangelistic testimony have demonstrated the glorious fact that civilization always follows in the wake of the story of the cross, and men learn to think kindlier of one another and to be concerned about the welfare of their fellows when the love of God is shed abroad in their hearts by the Holy Spirit who is given unto them.

To take the position, as many who are hailed as "great thinkers" do today, that we are not to be so much concerned about individual salvation as we are to seek the social regeneration of the nations, is to be false to our commission, and is a case of sadly misplaced emphasis. Man is made for eternity. His few years here on earth are but as a moment in contrast to that which lies beyond the grave. It is all important to every individual that he be properly oriented to his Creator—in other words, that he be right with God. Then all other necessary things will follow.

I recall hearing William Booth, the first general of the Salvation Army, say, when explaining his "Darkest England" scheme, that its real objective was, not just the amelioration of social conditions, but first and foremost the bringing of men to repentance that their souls might be saved. I can recall the flash in his eye, and the noble bearing of his commanding figure as he exclaimed, "Take a man from the filth and squalor of the slums, exchange his rags for decent clothing, move him from the stifling stench of the city tenement to a neat little cottage in the pure air of the country, put him on his feet economically where he can make a decent living for himself and his family, and then let him die in his sins, unsaved, and be lost forever at last—really it is not worthwhile, and I, for one, would not attempt it."

Godliness has "promise of the life that now is, and of that which is to come." But the only way one can enter into godliness is by turning to God as a repentant sinner and receiving the Saviour He has provided in the gospel. Therefore, the crying need of our degenerate times is for a revival of true, old-fashioned, Christ-centered, Bible preaching that will call on all men everywhere to repent in view of that coming day when God will judge the world in righteousness by His risen Son.

17
But is Repentance Desirable?

Now I come to discuss, in this closing chapter, what many will feel should have been the first question raised and settled: Is repentance, after all, desirable?

According to much of the humanistic thought of the day, there is no occasion whatever to call on mankind in general to repent. In fact, we are told, he who does so shows that he fails to appreciate man's innate dignity and praiseworthiness. The evolutionist points with pride to the abysmal depths of bestial ancestry from which man has struggled upward to his present exalted position. What some call sin is but the slowly conquered animal traits which, it may be hoped, will be outlived in future centuries. It is not for this magnificent, thinking creature to repent of anything, certainly not of his upward progress. If he condemns himself as a "miserable sinner," he fails to appreciate his glorious heritage. He is the child of all the ages; he has come the long, long way from a tiny speck of protoplasm to the dignity of a cultured Twentieth Century genius. Shall he repent that he is not what he once was? Does he not know that every fall has been a fall upward? Was it not by unceasing struggle with superstition, ignorance, and unwholesome environment that he has reached his present high estate? To command him to repent and to do works meet for repentance is to insult him to his face.

And then there are those who have given their adherence to various highly-lauded religious cults of widespread acceptance, all of which are based on the proposition that man is but a manifestation of God and that what the Bible calls sin is merely an "error of mortal mind." The realization of man's own Deity in order that he may

141

ever be "in tune with the Infinite," and so declare confidently, as Jesus did, that "I and my Father are one" will, we are told, enable us all to demonstrate the essential unity of the human spirit with the divine. But if this be so, there is no place for repentance. Repent of what—that I am one with God? Surely not. So these teachers, however much they may quarrel among themselves as to terms, all insist that the path of life and the way of peace are to ignore all that seems to be evil and to be occupied alone with the good and the true. "Condemn not thyself," is a favorite saying. And the devotees of all these systems consciously or unconsciously seek to build themselves up in spirituality and to rise to higher moral and ethical planes by means of constant repetition of the Coué formula,

> *"Every day, in every way,*
> *I am getting better and better."*

Of course, this kind of argument is only another form of the old and very familiar philosophy of the bootstrap. We do not have bootstraps on our shoes, but many act as if their minds had something of the kind and they were diligently trying to lift themselves to higher heights by pulling on them.

Often we are told that it is degrading and belittling to cry, "Repent!" We should rather shout, Advance! and, forgetting the past, reach forth to the better things the future has in store. Did not Paul tell us this in his Philippian letter? The answer is, he did not. He himself tells us in that very epistle how he once gloried in his fleshly religion until the vision of the risen Christ brought him to repentance, so that what things were gain to him he now counted but as dross in order that He who had manifested Himself to him might henceforth be magnified in him, whether by life or death. Now he could forget the things behind and reach forth in holy expectation to the things beyond, "the prize of the high calling of God in Christ Jesus."

For nearly a century the world has been drinking at the fount of these strange philosophies, and one might have thought that by now, if they were true at all, we would see a great improvement in the human race. But lust, cruelty, corruption, and violence were never more prominent than in these strangely unsettled years since the close of the World War—the war that was to end all war and henceforth make the world safe for democracy. But the nations are still in turmoil, showing that the nations are far from realizing the idealism in which their salvation is supposed to be assured.

No, man is not God-like. He is not at one with the Infinite mind. He is not a great, heroic figure dominating the ages. He is a poor, needy, sinful creature who will never find the path of peace until he humbles himself before high Heaven and repentantly confesses his manifold iniquities. He must look to the cross of Christ and to the Holy Spirit of God for twofold deliverance—justification before God and practical santification of life. All this must be through the power of the Word applied by Him who alone produces a second birth and comes to indwell all who believe in the Lord Jesus Christ to the salvation of their souls.

Applied psychology, psychiatry, and ethical culture, will not bring this about. Whatever value there may be in the wise use of these systems, so far as combating certain conditions of the mind is concerned, they are utterly powerless to change the heart of man or to produce a new life. J. R. Oliver, in a volume entitled *Psychiatry and Mental Health*, frankly confesses that, after all, the varied needs of mankind can best be met by "the divine Psychiatrist, the one great Physician of the soul." He rightly declares that if we know Him and walk with Him, all books on mental science, moral theology, marriage and birth control, with all the well-meant regulatory laws which have been tried or proposed to curb the evil desires of men and nations, could be safely discarded, for in Christ is found all that is needed to give us moral and spiritual health. To turn to Jesus as the Great Physician is to repent, for He came to heal—not the well—but the sick. His message was for those who had lost their way. What His enemies said of Him in derision and contempt is blessedly true and the cause for everlasting praise, "This Man receiveth sinners, and eateth with them."

But so long as men insist on attempting to justify themselves and

143

their behavior, they are under the divine condemnation. It is concerning him who cries, 'I have sinned and perverted that which was right and it profiteth me not,' that the voice of God exclaims, "Deliver him from going down to the pit; I have found a ransom." (see Job 33:14-30). We are told in Psalm 76:10, "Surely the wrath of man shall praise Thee: the remainder of wrath shalt Thou restrain." It is another way of saying that all confessed sin shall be made to serve in the working out of God's eternal purpose. Where recognized guilt leads to repentance, the forgiven man rises to a consciously higher plane than he would otherwise have attained. Our sin becomes the dark background that better displays the lustrous jewel of divine grace. We know God better as forgiven sinners than Adam knew Him, as unfallen in that first earthly Paradise. It is this that makes the joy of heaven so great, as the redeemed adore the Lamb and sing His praises who was slain in order that He might wash us from our sins in His own blood. Not one voice in that wondrous choir will attribute merit to other than Christ Himself.

In a recent book, in which one was objecting to expressions such as these, the writer challenged those who habitually confess themselves miserable sinners and acknowledge that they have left undone the things they ought to have done and done the things they ought not to have done, to dare to say such derogatory things of themselves when applying for a position of trust in some reputable firm. The implication was that if such language was not suited as between man and man, it was not proper between man and God.

One does not have to be a "deep thinker" to see the fallacy of this. A man is hired by a firm because of his supposed ability and trustworthiness. But men's standards are altogether different from those set forth in the Holy Scriptures. Righteousness is emphasized in our dealings with our fellowmen; holiness when it comes to relationship with God. A man's life may be outwardly correct and righteous, while his heart is corrupt and unholy. "The Lord seeth not as man seeth; for man looketh on the outward appearance, but the Lord looketh on the heart." He desires truth in the inward parts.

It is the pure in heart who shall see God. Therefore the absolute

144

necessity of the new birth, apart from which there can be no spiritual enlightenment. The heart of the natural man is as a nest of every unclean and hateful bird; all sorts of evils come forth from it. The mind of the unsaved man is incapable of grasping heavenly realities. His understanding is darkened because of the ignorance that is in him. When he accepts God's testimony, he takes the position of repentance, and is in an attitude where God can reveal to him the wonders of redeeming grace. In no other way can guilty man be reconciled to God, who beholds the proud afar off, but is near to every broken and contrite heart.

If these pages fall into the hands of any anxious, troubled soul who desire to find the way of peace, and earnestly seeking to be right with God, let me urge you to give up all struggling. Just believe God. Tell Him you are the sinner for whom the Saviour died, and trust in Christ alone for salvation. His own word is clear and simple: "Verily, verily I say unto you, He that heareth My word, and believeth on Him that sent Me, hath everlasting life, and shall not come into condemnation; but is passed from death into life" (Jn. 5:24).

To hear the Word is to receive God's testimony, and this is the very essence of repentance. When anyone who has spurned that Word bows to its message, even though it tells him he is lost and undone and has no righteousness of his own, he turns from his vain thoughts and accepts instead the testimony of the Lord. It is to such that the Holy Spirit delights to present a crucified, risen, and exalted Christ as the one supreme object of faith. He who trusts Him is forever freed from all condemnation (see Jn. 3:18). He is immediately safe in Christ, and "There is therefore now no condemnation to them that are in Christ Jesus" (Rom. 8:1).

This is not to say his own conscience will never again condemn him, for that is not true. The nearer he lives to his Lord, the more tender his conscience will be. But it does mean that God no longer sees him as a sinner exposed to judgment, but that He counts him, from then on, as a child, a member of the heavenly family, accepted in Christ, the beloved of the Father.

In this blessed relationship, the believer has by no means finished with repentance. He is called on daily to judge himself in the light of the Word of Truth, as it is opened up to him by the Spirit, and so to repent of anything that he learns to be contrary to the mind of God. Otherwise he will have to know the Father's chastening rod. "For if we would judge ourselves, we should not be judged. But when we are judged, we are chastened of the Lord, that we should not be condemned with the world" (1 Cor. 11:31-32). It is in view of this that He says, "Be zealous therefore, and repent."

But I must bring these remarks to a conclusion. I need not multiply words. This book is, perhaps, already much too lengthy for busy readers, though I hope many will take time to examine carefully, in the light of the Holy Scriptures, every position taken. The conclusion of the whole matter is simply this: Repentance is not only desirable, but it is imperative and all important. Apart from it, no sinner will ever be saved. God Himself commands all men everywhere to repent. Our Lord Jesus declared, "Except ye repent, ye shall all likewise perish." That which it is so perilous to neglect should be faithfully preached to all for whom Christ died. And when men receive the message in faith and judge themselves in the light of the cross, they may know that all heaven resounds with gladness for "there is joy in the presence of the angels of God over one sinner that repenteth" (Lk. 15:10).

The glorified throng in heaven will all be there, not because they were holier or in any way better in themselves than other men, but because, as repentant sinners, they "washed their robes, and made them white in the blood of the Lamb." He alone will be extolled as the Worthy One. All who are ever saved will be saved through His merits alone.

A Brief Historical Sketch

To understand the importance of this book, it seems right that we know to whom H. A. Ironside was directing his remarks.

Beginning in 1924, Ironside lectured for two months to the students of Dallas Theological Seminary (then known as Evangelical Theological College) in Dallas, Texas. This arrangement continued for several years. Lewis Sperry Chafer (1871-1952), president of the seminary, was anxious to have Ironside join the faculty. An offer was made, which Ironside refused. However, he did accept from Chafer the position of a member of the Board of Regents at the seminary in 1929. His son, Edmund, attended the Dallas school, and Ironside continued to annually lecture there, to within two years of his death. He admired and loved brother Chafer, and would not want to have done anything to damage their valued fellowship. But on the issue of repentance, he disagreed. It could be said that this book on repentance was written to keep Chafer honest.

Some think of Chafer as an academic, solely absorbed in Bible teaching, secluded in his seminary library. This was not true. He and his wife were zealous soul winners, especially in their early ministry. When Chafer spoke on evangelism to his students, he was able, from his own personal experience, to relate numerous instances of God's guidance and blessing on his gospel preaching. He was a gifted, intelligent, and ardent personal worker who dreaded shallow emotionalism and spurious conversions. Acquaintants and confidants alike knew him as a man of God.

Chafer was also a thorough disciple of Cyrus Ingerson Scofield (1843-1921), and when the fundamentalists endorsed C. I. Scofield's approach to dispensationalism, outlined in the Scofield

Reference Bible, they also largely accepted his view of repentance. Chafer embraced these views and became their most effective advocate. This is reflected in Chafer's treatment of the doctrine in his *Systematic Theology*. For instance, in Volume III, Chafer says that repentance is something that those already in a Covenant relationship to God, such as the Old Testament Jews and present-day Christians should do, but that "there is no basis either in reason or revelation for the demand to be made that an unregenerate person in this age must add a covenant person's repentance to faith in order to be saved" (p. 376). And in the section on "THE ABSENCE OF THE DEMAND FOR REPENTANCE FROM SALVATION SCRIPTURES," Chafer says "From this overwhelming mass of irrefutable evidence, it is clear that the New Testament does not impose repentance upon the unsaved as a condition of salvation" (p. 376). Generally when Chafer came to passages which refuted his "irrefutable evidence," saying that unregenerate people are to repent, such as Luke 24:47 or Acts 11:18, he countered that "repentance, which is included in believing, serves as a synonym for the word *belief*" (p. 377).

So Chafer did concede that the lost are to repent, but he so defined the lost person's repentance as to divorce it from the idea of turning from sin. Interestingly, when Chafer dealt with the Prodigal Son, his aversion to telling the lost to repent of sin forced him to the conclusion that the prodigal could not picture a lost sinner, but rather a backslidden child of God. Chafer taught scores of students such things, who in turn have influenced the evangelical world with a doctrinal view whose end result has reduced faith to a purely mental ascent. Today this doctrine is popularly called "easy believism."

At the beginning of the fundamentalist movement, there stood another pillar beside C. I. Scofield. He had been Dwight L. Moody's right-hand man. His name was Rueben Archer Torrey (1856-1928). Torrey and Scofield had differences dotrinally, one of which was the way they handled the teaching of Jesus Christ on repentance and the place of repentance in the preaching of the gospel.

R. A. Torrey succeeded D. L. Moody in the pulpit of Moody's congregation in Chicago—the same pulpit which H. A. Ironside would eventually occupy. As the director of the summer Montrose Bible Conference in Pennsylvania, Torrey invited Ironside to speak there, and, in 1930, Ironside succeeded Torrey as director.

The importance of this snatch of history for us today is to see that from the start there were two very different views on this vital topic at the roots of the fundamentalist movement. The one view, championed by C. I. Scofield and later systematically taught by Lewis Sperry Chafer, seems to almost dread using the word "repent" and handles the topic similar to the way in which a donkey eats thistles—very carefully.

The other view was championed by R. A. Torrey, as you would find him dealing with the need for repentance in his book, *How to Bring Men to Christ.* H. A. Ironside was not a clone of Torrey. But on this particular point, they were in whole-hearted agreement. Ironside did not speak on repentance with the guarded hesitancy of a man unsure of his footing. In the book, *The Unchanging Christ,* he preached the message, *How Pilate Lost His Soul,* and in the book, *God's Unspeakable Gift,* he preached the messages on *How Herod Lost His Soul* and *How Judas Iscariot Lost His Soul.* In these messages, Ironside showed that these men failed to repent of particular sins, and therefore perished.

Ironside was uniquely qualified to give this clarion call. He was first a fruitful evangelist, who had dealt with souls in close quarters, and secondly, he was a thorough, intelligent Bible teacher. Besides this, Ironside was a man of unimpeachable orthodoxy, whose work continues to command the respect of the Church of God. He was called the Archbishop of Fundamentalism, and if anyone was in a position to see the drift of the evangelical church, he was.

When you compare the forceful Bible teaching of H. A. Ironside in this book to the cursory explanations in Chafer's *Systematic Theology,* it tells a story of its own. Those who minimize the place of repentance in their preaching, or worse, banish it altogether, are left with very scant standing ground after reading this book.

JOHN A. BJORLIE

Subject Index

SUBJECT INDEX

155

Scripture Index